BIBLE ADVENTURE STORIES

25 Inspiring and Easy to Understand Bible Stories for Kids

BOOK 1

BIBLE ADVENTURERS

Copyright © 2015 Herobrine Publishing

All rights reserved. No part of this publication may be reproduced, distributed, or transmitted in any form or by any means, electronic or mechanical, including photocopying, recording, scanning, or by any information storage or retrieval system, without the prior written permission of the publisher, except in the case of brief quotations embodied in critical reviews and certain other non-commercial uses permitted by copyright law.

THE STORY OF CREATION

GENESIS CHAPTERS 1-2

Do you know where people came from or how the universe was made?

We haven't always been here and we certainly didn't make ourselves!

This is the story of how God created everything in only seven days. I know that sounds like a short time, but God is so powerful, He can do cool things like that.

Before there were stars or planets, or even people, there was just dark empty space as far as the eye could see. If you've ever woken up in the middle of the night, and noticed how dark it was, you know what I'm talking about.

Now, because God is creative, one day He decided He wanted to create something amazing. So, the first thing God did was create the universe. Now, as you probably know, the universe is the place where all the stars and galaxies are. And the universe is really big. It's so big that there are almost one hundred billion galaxies in the universe. Yeah, I know…that's huge.

But, let's get back to our story…

God also created all the planets. Then He created the ultimate planet and called it earth, because it would be the home for every human being. In other words, when God was thinking of the most fun place for us to live and play in, He created the amazing planet earth to be our playground.

Now, when He first created the earth, it was round and empty, kind of like a big rubber ball. Actually, it was dark and covered with water, because He hadn't created light or land yet.

God created light so that it wouldn't be so dark all the time. And He called the light "day." Then, He split half the day and made it light, and made the other half dark. And by doing this He created the daytime and He created the night time.

And He did all of that on the first day. Yeah, God had a really busy first day.

BIBLE ADVENTURE STORIES

On the second day, God decided that He wanted to create the sky. So He spent the second day creating the sky above the earth.

Now, I'm sure God had a reason for making the sky blue. It could be that blue is God's favorite color. Or it could be that He thought that a red sky might be too intense for people. Or maybe He thought that a polka dot sky would be weird. I don't know why He did it, but I'm sure He must've had a good reason. When we get to heaven, I guess we can ask Him.

On the third day, God decided that He wanted more than just water covering the earth, so He made the ground and called it "land." Then He made all the plants and trees that grow on the ground. God created everything from the giant redwood trees to the Venus flytrap.

God looked at everything He had created and said, "Yeah, this is good!"

I told you God was creative.

On the fourth day, God made the sun and the moon. He had the sun shine during the day and the moon to shine at night.

BIBLE ADVENTURE STORIES

…and, no, He didn't make the moon out of cheese.

Then He made all the stars in the universe for us to enjoy and marvel at. It's kind of like God was preparing our room, with those cool stick-on stars on the ceiling, so that when we look up at night, we'd be like, "Cool!"

After He finished, He looked at it and said, "This is really good!"

On the fifth day, God made the fish and other creatures that live in water. So He made everything from the octopus to the giant blue whale.

God made all the cool birds too, like eagles and vultures, parakeets and even bats. Though I tricked you because bats are not birds, they're mammals, and they came the next day.

On the sixth day, God created all the creatures that live on the earth, like horses, cows and wild animals. And yes, He made snakes and cockroaches, and worms and spiders. I really don't know why He created the creepy crawly things, but he did, so I'm sure he had a good reason.

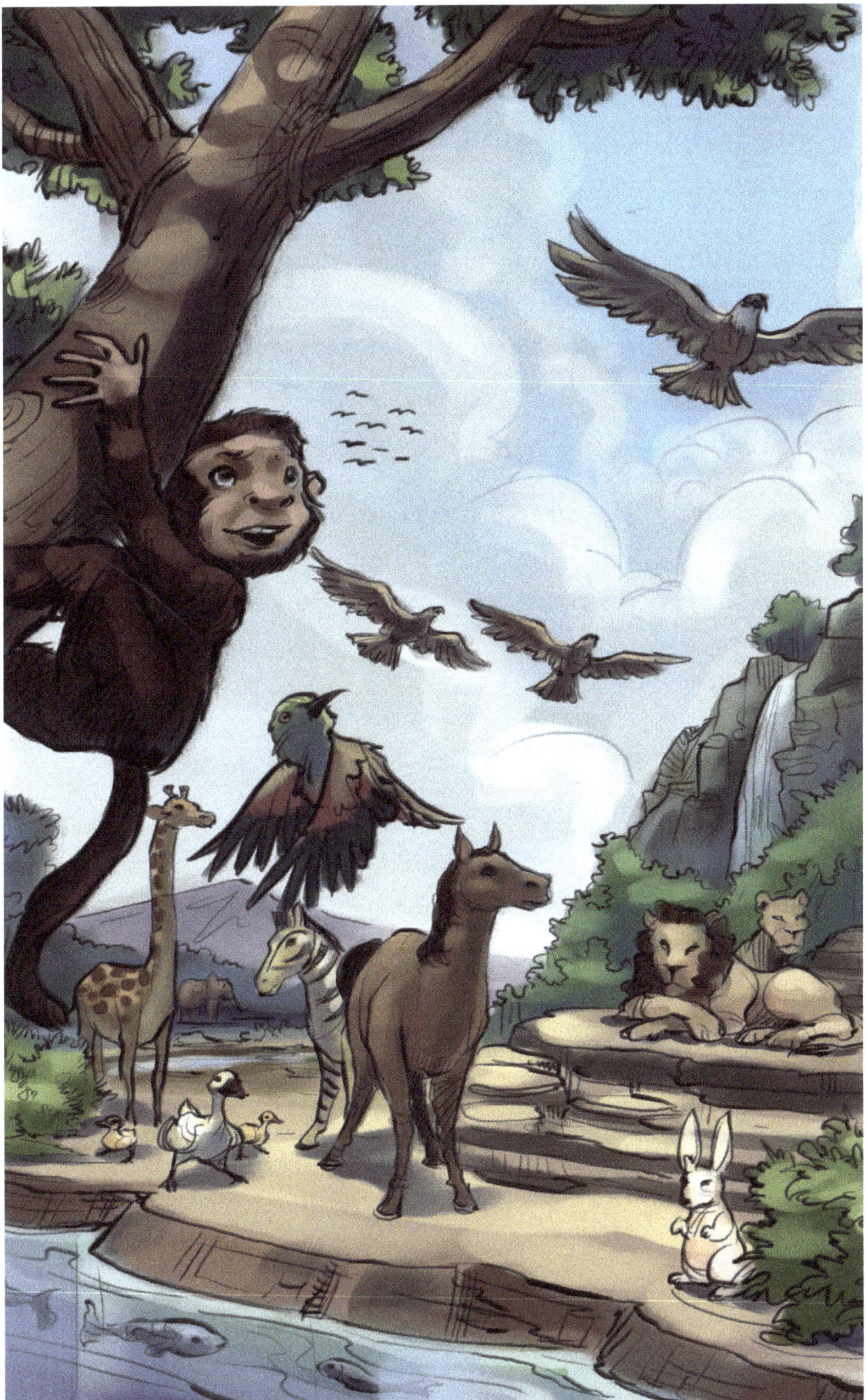

BIBLE ADVENTURE STORIES

And most important of all, on that sixth day, God made people. He made a man and He made a woman.

He made the first man out of the dirt on the ground. Now, I don't know why He made us out of dirt, but I guess it's better than making us out of trees. If we were made from trees, hugging other people would probably hurt, a lot.

Then God breathed life into man and called him Adam. Now He could've called him Rory or Erol or something like that, or maybe even Zack. But, I guess if the first man was named Egbert, this story wouldn't be as exciting.

Then he let Adam name all the animals. I think it was probably because God wanted to share some of the work. I'm sure creating a brand new world takes a lot of effort. Though, I don't think Adam had a lot of training. I'm still trying to understand where he came up with a weird name like Platypus.

Now, God noticed that Adam was lonely so He put him into a deep sleep and used one of his ribs to make a woman. He called her Eve. I kind of wonder, though, what Eve would've looked like if God used Adam's foot instead.

And do you know what God did on the seventh day? He spent the day just enjoying what He created. Kind of like when you make something really cool out of Legos, and you look back and think, "Wow, that is awesome!"

I guess since we are God's creation, God is looking at us and He's thinking we're really awesome too.

It's great to know that God is so powerful that he can create the entire universe in seven days. It's also really good to know that he's looking down on us right now, and he's really happy with his work.

> *I will give thanks to You, for I am fearfully and wonderfully made; Wonderful are Your works, And my soul knows it very well.*
>
> **Psalms 139:14**
> **NASB**

NOAH AND THE ARK

GENESIS CHAPTERS 6-8

Do you know what happens when you leave a bunch of kids to run around and do whatever they want?

That's right. Everything goes nuts!

Well, after many years, the people on the earth decided that instead of following God they were going to do whatever they wanted. And of course, the world went nuts!

When God saw what people were doing, it really hurt him a lot. Especially when He saw his children hurting each other.

So God decided to flood the whole world and start all over.

Now, it wasn't because He made a mistake the first time. To be honest, I don't know why He did it. But I can imagine it was probably because there were too many evil people in the world.

You see, by the time God was ready to flood the world, there was only one man in the whole world that followed God and did what was right. And his name was Noah.

That's pretty amazing when you think about how many people were in the world. But no matter how crazy the world got, Noah continued to love God and obey him. The bible says that Noah was the most righteous man on earth.

Another special thing about Noah was that he had a best friend. And his best friend was God. The bible says that Noah walked with God. That's like when you hang out with your friends. You guys spend time together, talk together, have fun together or just hang out together. This is how Noah was with God.

So when God decided to flood the world, God decided to save his friend Noah. And I think as a favor to Noah, He saved his family too.

God also wanted to save two of all living creatures, both male and female. This is because when God was ready to start all over, he would have animals he could start from. I guess this included insects and spiders too. Or, maybe they just hitched along for the ride.

Now, since God was going to flood the earth, He had to find a way to save Noah and his family, and all of the animals. God could've created a submarine to save Noah and his family. But God decided an ark would probably be a better idea. I guess that makes sense, because with all those animals, a submarine would've gotten pretty smelly, very quickly.

So God told Noah to build an ark. And this ark was huge. It was 450 feet long, 75 feet wide and 45 feet high. It was bigger than a football field, and almost as big as the Titanic.

That's a pretty big boat for one guy to build. But Noah did it. So the next time you think about how hard it is to clean your room, think of Noah.

When Noah finally finished the ark, all of a sudden two of every animal in the world came from everywhere and walked into the ark all by themselves! We're talking lions, bears, camels, elephants, gorillas, giraffes, dogs, cats, mice, emus, the platypus, and more…

That's pretty amazing when you think about it. But with God, you know it's going to be amazing.

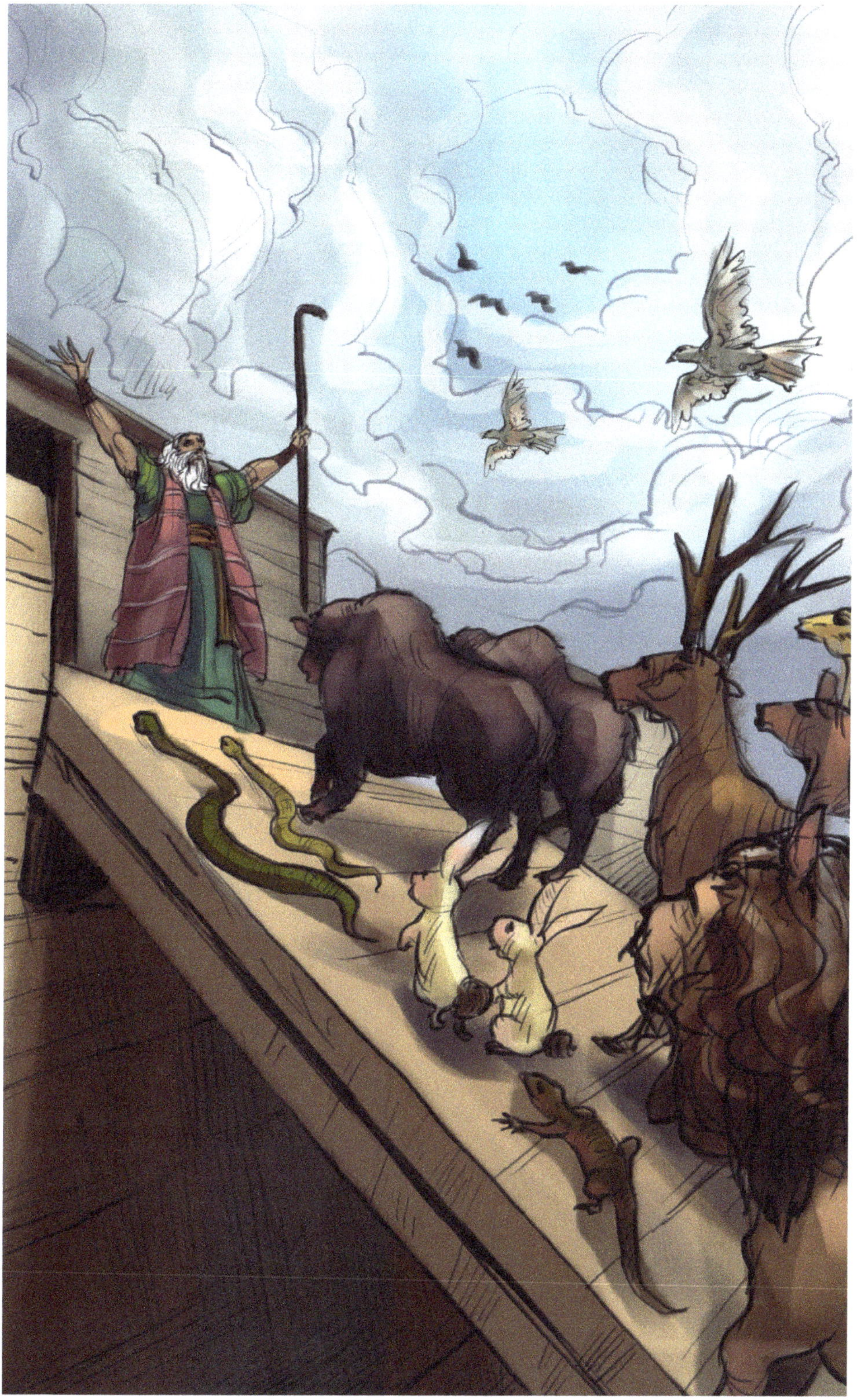

Later, when the last animal walked into the ark, and Noah and his family entered the ark, God closed the doors.

Then God opened the flood gates both on the ground and in the sky. Water gushed up out of the ocean floor, and water poured down out of the sky. It was so much water that it covered the entire earth. Now, that's a lot of water!

Some people have a hard time understanding how God could make it rain all around the world at the same time. Or, people wonder how God could flood the whole world at the same time. But I guess that's what makes God, you know…God. He could do stuff like that. You see, unlike us, God has unlimited power and so He could do anything He wants.

I'm just glad He's on our side…

The rain God sent kept pouring from the sky for forty days and forty nights. And, you're probably wondering how Noah kept all those animals happy for so many days in the ark. Some people think that God may have put them all to sleep, like when bears hibernate for the winter. But I know what you are probably thinking, and the answer is no, bears don't poop while they're hibernating.

So, altogether, the earth was flooded for a hundred and fifty days. But, God didn't forget about Noah. He sent a wind to evaporate the flood water from over all the earth. I know, that must've been some powerful wind.

After most of the water had evaporated, Noah's Ark landed on the Mountain of Ararat. And, after a few more weeks, Noah opened a window and looked out. When he looked out, he could see the tops of some mountains, so he knew the water was going down.

A few weeks later, Noah sent out a raven to see if it would find a place to live. He knew that if the raven didn't come back, then it found a tree where it could build a nest. This also meant that the flood water was gone.

But, the raven came back. A week later he sent out a dove to see if it could find a place to live. But it came back too. Then the week after, he sent out the dove again, but this time it came back with a fresh leaf in its beak! And a week after that, he sent the dove out again to find a home, but this time it didn't come back. So Noah knew the earth was dry.

God told Noah that the time was right to come out of the ark. So Noah and his family, and all of the animals, came out of the ark.

BIBLE ADVENTURE STORIES

Noah built an altar to God, and he burnt sacrifices on it. I know this sounds kind of weird, but this is the way that people showed their appreciation to God in Noah's day. Kind of like when your parents have a barbeque to celebrate 4th of July or some holiday like that.

After Noah worshipped God, God promised that He would never flood the world ever again. And to remind everyone about his promise, He created the rainbow and put it in the sky. So whenever you see a rainbow, that is God reminding you that He loves you and that He will never flood the world ever again.

> *By faith, Noah built a ship in the middle of dry land. He was warned about something he couldn't see, and acted on what he was told. The result? His family was saved.*
>
> **Hebrews 11:7**
> **MSG**

MOSES AND THE PLAGUES

EXODUS CHAPTER 5-12

Many years after Noah, God chose a group of people called the Israelites to be his own special people. He chose them because He wanted a group of people He could show his love to and that would love Him back. He took care of the needs of His people, He blessed his people with great gifts, and He protected them and kept them safe from danger.

This is kind of like how our Mom and Dad take care of us, watch over us, help us, and protect us from danger. God was like a father to the Israelites, and they were his children.

By taking care of His people like this, God wanted His people to be an example to the rest of the world. He wanted to show the world that they could have a loving relationship with Him too. This is because God wants to have a relationship with every single person in the entire world…Including you.

BIBLE ADVENTURE STORIES

But something happened to his people. After many years, the Israelites became ungrateful, and stopped obeying God. They started to forget that God was the one that had blessed them and helped them, and they started to think that they did it themselves. Sadly, they forgot God, they stopped loving God and they stopped obeying him.

So, like a loving father, God wanted to remind his people to be grateful. If you've ever met a spoiled person, you know how bad they can be. And God knew that if his children continued to live like that they wouldn't make it to heaven. And He couldn't have that!

So God had to discipline his people and teach them how to be grateful again. The way God did this was to stop providing for his people, stop blessing His people and stop protecting His people from danger.

Now, the Israelites were living in Egypt at the time. The rulers of Egypt, called the Pharaohs, were really mean. So when the Israelites stopped obeying God, God stopped protecting them from the rulers of Egypt. Eventually, the mean rulers of Egypt oppressed the Israelites and made them into their slaves.

So for many years the Israelite slaves were treated really badly by the Egyptians. When the Israelites couldn't take it anymore, they started to cry out to God and apologize to Him for forgetting Him, and for not loving and obeying him.

God heard their cry and He felt really bad for them. That's because even though He had to discipline them, He still loved his people very much.

So God sent them a hero, called Moses, to go and save them.

God appeared to Moses one day in a burning bush and asked him to go save his people and lead them out of Egypt. God planned to work his miracles through Moses and convince the Egyptian Pharaoh to let his people go.

But Moses didn't want to go. When you think about it, who would? God was asking Moses to go into Egypt and to tell the mean Egyptian ruler to let their millions of slaves go free. Not the easiest task in the world.

But God promised Moses that He would be with him. He also told Moses to take his brother Aaron so he wouldn't be alone on his quest.

So Moses went to Pharaoh, the mean Egyptian king, to tell him to let God's people go. Pharaoh wasn't too happy about it, so of course, he said no.

Moses told Pharaoh that if he didn't let God's people go that God was going to send plagues on Egypt until Pharaoh freed God's people. Now, a plague is a really bad event, like a sickness or a problem that hurts a lot of people.

But Pharaoh didn't believe him. So Moses left, and God sent plagues on Egypt until Pharaoh decided to let his people, the Israelites, go.

God first sent a plague that turned all of the water in Egypt into blood. Even the water in their cups and their jugs was turned to blood. Imagine, they couldn't take a bath or drink because all the water was turned to blood.

When this happened, Pharaoh told Moses that he would let God's people go if he would make the plague go away. So Moses prayed to God to make the plague go away, and God did it. Then Moses asked Pharaoh to let God's people go, but Pharaoh changed his mind and said no.

After that, God sent a plague of frogs that would make frogs come out of the river and infest their land. All of a sudden, thousands of frogs came out of the river and completely covered Egypt. Imagine, they had frogs in their shoes, frogs in their shirts and pants, frogs in their drawers and frogs in their sinks and bathtubs. Gross.

When this happened, Pharaoh told Moses that he would let God's people go if he would make the plague go away. So Moses prayed to God again to make the plague go away, and God did it. Then Moses asked Pharaoh to let God's people go, but Pharaoh changed his mind again and said no.

Then God sent plague after plague to the land of Egypt to make Pharaoh let God's people go free. But every time it happened, Pharaoh would first say yes, that he would let the Israelites go, but then after the plague was gone, he changed his mind and said no.

God sent all kinds of plagues on Egypt. He sent plagues of gnats (or lice, eeew!), flies, disease on their livestock (like their cows, and sheep), and boils (which are giant, painful pimples that grew all over their bodies, yuck!).

God also sent a plague of thunder, a plague of hail (which are like giant baseball sized ice balls that fell from the sky), a plague of locusts that covered the sky, and a plague of darkness.

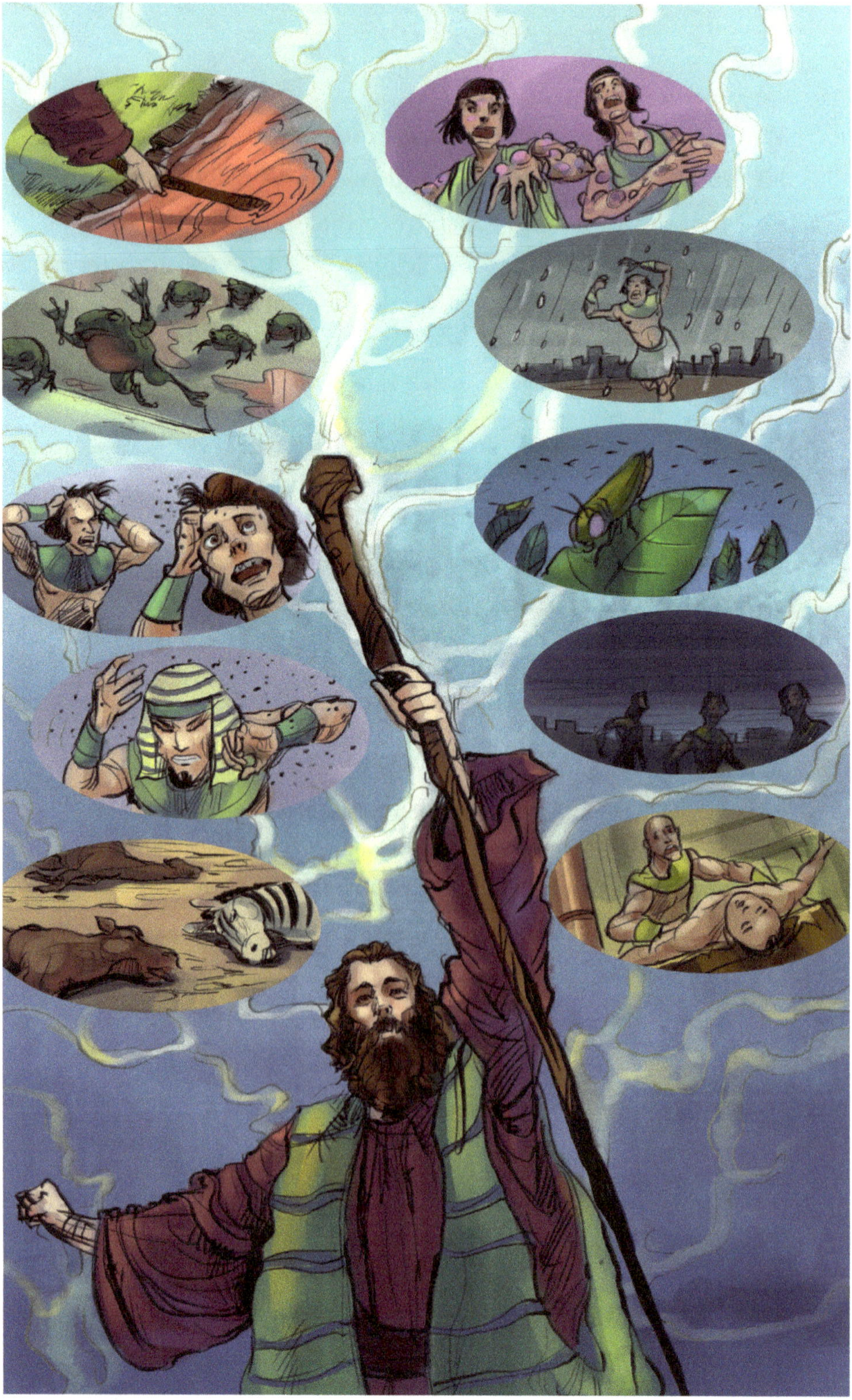

But Pharaoh kept promising that he was going to let the Israelites go free, yet when the plague was gone, he would change his mind.

If you've ever had somebody promise you they were going to do something, and later they change their mind, you probably know how Moses felt when Pharaoh kept changing his mind.

Finally, Moses told Pharaoh that God was going to send the worst plague ever to the land of Egypt. He told Pharaoh that God was going to send an angel of death to kill the first born son of every family in Egypt. I guess by this point, God had had enough. He was going to show Pharaoh how serious he really was.

But before God sent the plague, God wanted to make sure that the angel of death didn't hurt the first born sons of the Israelites. So God told Moses to tell the Israelites living in Egypt to put blood over the door frames of their houses. This way, when the angel of death came, he would pass over the houses of the Israelites and not touch their sons. And if you didn't know, this is actually where the holiday called Passover comes from; when the angel of death passed over the houses of the Israelites and spared their sons.

Later, after the angel of death passed through Egypt, Pharaoh finally realized that God was serious. Pharaoh finally kept his promise to let the Israelites go free.

So Moses led millions of Israelites out of Egypt and led them to a new home that God promised them.

But this wasn't the last time they would hear from Pharaoh…

> *"If you'll hold on to me for dear life," says God, "I'll get you out of any trouble. I'll give you the best of care if you'll only get to know and trust me.*
>
> **Psalms 91:14**
> **MSG**

MOSES AND THE ISRAELITES CROSS THE RED SEA

EXODUS CHAPTERS 13-15

Now, after the Israelites left Egypt, Pharaoh got really mad and changed his mind, again! He decided that he was going to go after the Israelites, capture them, and make them slaves all over again. So he mustered every soldier in his army and all of his chariots to go after the Israelites.

The Israelites were really happy that God saved them and that He led them out of Egypt. They were really grateful that when they needed help they called out to God, and He came to their rescue.

But when they got to the Red Sea, they had to find boats to cross over because they didn't have any. All of a sudden they heard a loud rumbling noise. They looked behind them and saw that the entire Egyptian army was coming after them!

They were so scared that they started to complain to Moses that he should've never led them out of Egypt. But Moses encouraged them to trust in God.

Moses said to the people, "Do not be afraid. Stand firm and you will see the deliverance the LORD will bring you today. The Egyptians you see today you will never see again. The LORD will fight for you; you need only to be still."

So Moses prayed to God and asked him for help. God told Moses to just raise his hands, and God would save his people from the Egyptians.

So Moses raised both of his hands, and all of a sudden, a massive wind came and started blowing on the water of the Red Sea. The wind blew so hard that it made the Red Sea split in half! There was a wall of water on one side and a wall of water on the other side.

Then Moses told the Israelites to hurry and walk through the Red Sea to get to the other side. So the Israelites walked through the Red sea on dry ground, because God separated the Red Sea so that the Israelites could cross.

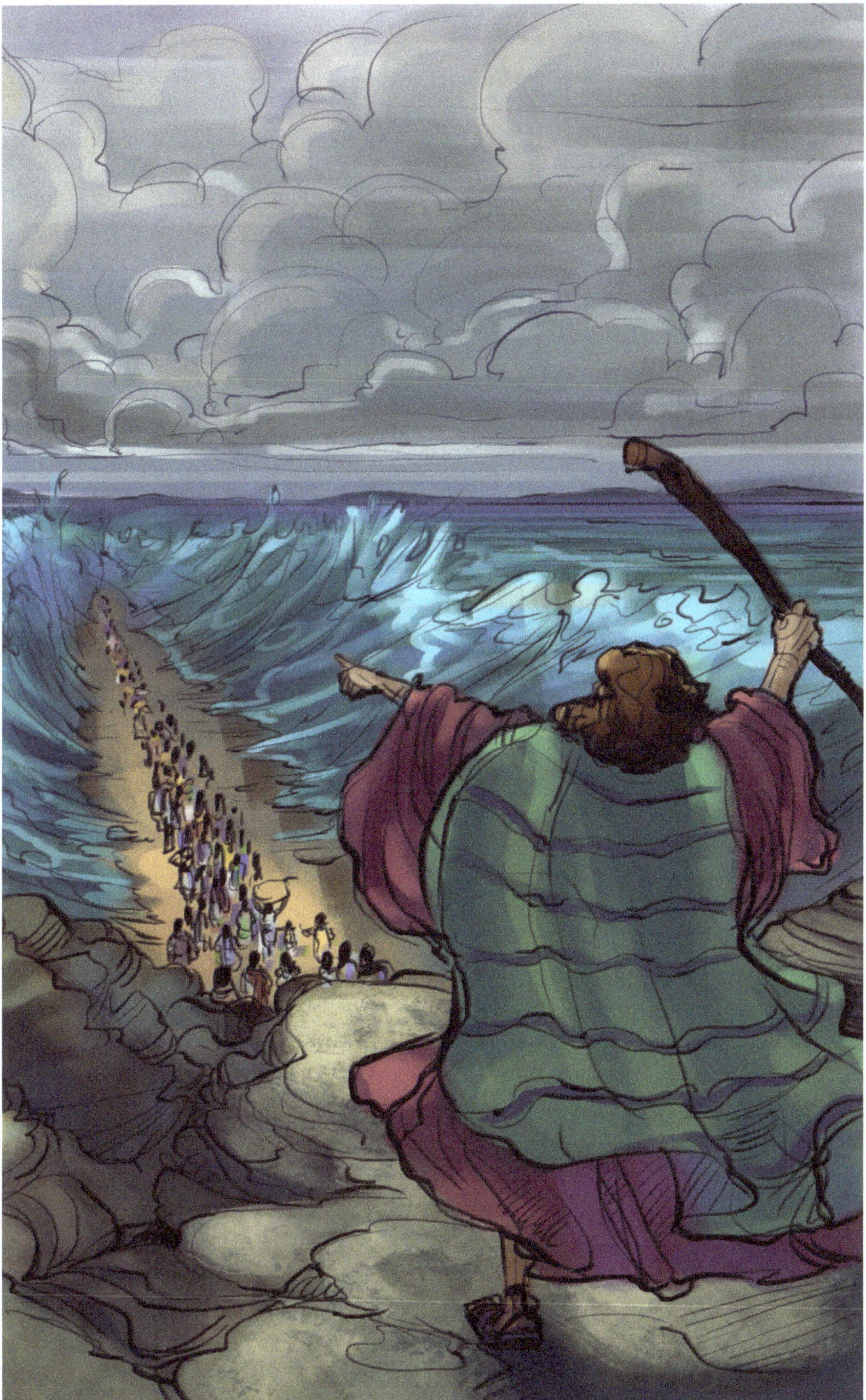

BIBLE ADVENTURE STORIES

The Egyptians chased after the Israelites straight into the Red Sea. And when the final Israelite got out of the Red Sea, God made the walls of the Red Sea come crashing down onto the Egyptian army and drowned them all.

So God saved the Israelites and allowed them to cross the Red Sea on dry ground.

> *[God says]"Don't be afraid, I've redeemed you. I've called your name. You're mine. When you're in over your head, I'll be there with you. When you're in rough waters, you will not go down.*
>
> **Isaiah 43: 1–2**
> **MSG**

JOSHUA AND THE WALL OF JERICHO

JOSHUA CHAPTER 6

Years later, after the Israelites crossed the Red Sea, Moses chose an assistant named Joshua. Joshua helped Moses do all of the things that God commanded him.

By now, Moses was very old. But before Moses died, God told Moses that Joshua would lead the Israelites into a place called Canaan, known as the Promised Land. It was supposed to be a really nice place where the Israelites could live and raise their families.

Unfortunately, there were really evil people that lived in Canaan. God wanted to remove these evil people from Canaan before He would let his people settle in the Promised Land. He didn't want his people to move there until He knew the city was safe.

So after Moses died, God sent Joshua and his fighting men into Canaan to a place called Jericho to get rid of these bad men. But the men of Jericho had a strong fortress, with really thick walls that no one could penetrate.

Joshua and his men had to find a way to get into Jericho, but they couldn't think of any. So, Joshua asked God for help.

Now you would think that God would send a powerful angel to help them, or send a lightning bolt to destroy the fortress, or something like that, right? Instead, God just told them to march around the city once for six days, and on the seventh day, He told them to march around the city seven times. By doing that, God promised them that the walls of the city of Jericho would come down.

Now, I don't know about you, but I would probably be thinking, "What is God talking about? Walk around the city and the walls will come down? That's crazy! How's that going to do anything?"

But because Joshua trusted God, he did it anyway. So, for six days he and his men marched around the city once.

Now, I'm sure the people in Jericho were probably laughing at them for doing something as silly as walking around Jericho every day. Maybe they were even throwing rocks or rotten fruit at them from the walls.

"Ha, Ha! What are you going to do? Walk us to death?" they probably said. Or, "Aren't your feet hurting by now?" Or "I thought you guys were fighters, not tourists."

Then on the seventh day, Joshua got up early with his men, and they walked around the city seven times. They must've been really tired, and their feet must've hurt, a lot.

But, after they finished walking, Joshua told his men to blow their trumpets and shout! And Joshua's army did. They all blew their trumpets and shouted at the top of their lungs.

Suddenly, they heard a rumbling sound. Then they heard a cracking sound. Then out of nowhere, the thick powerful walls of the fortress of Jericho came crashing down.

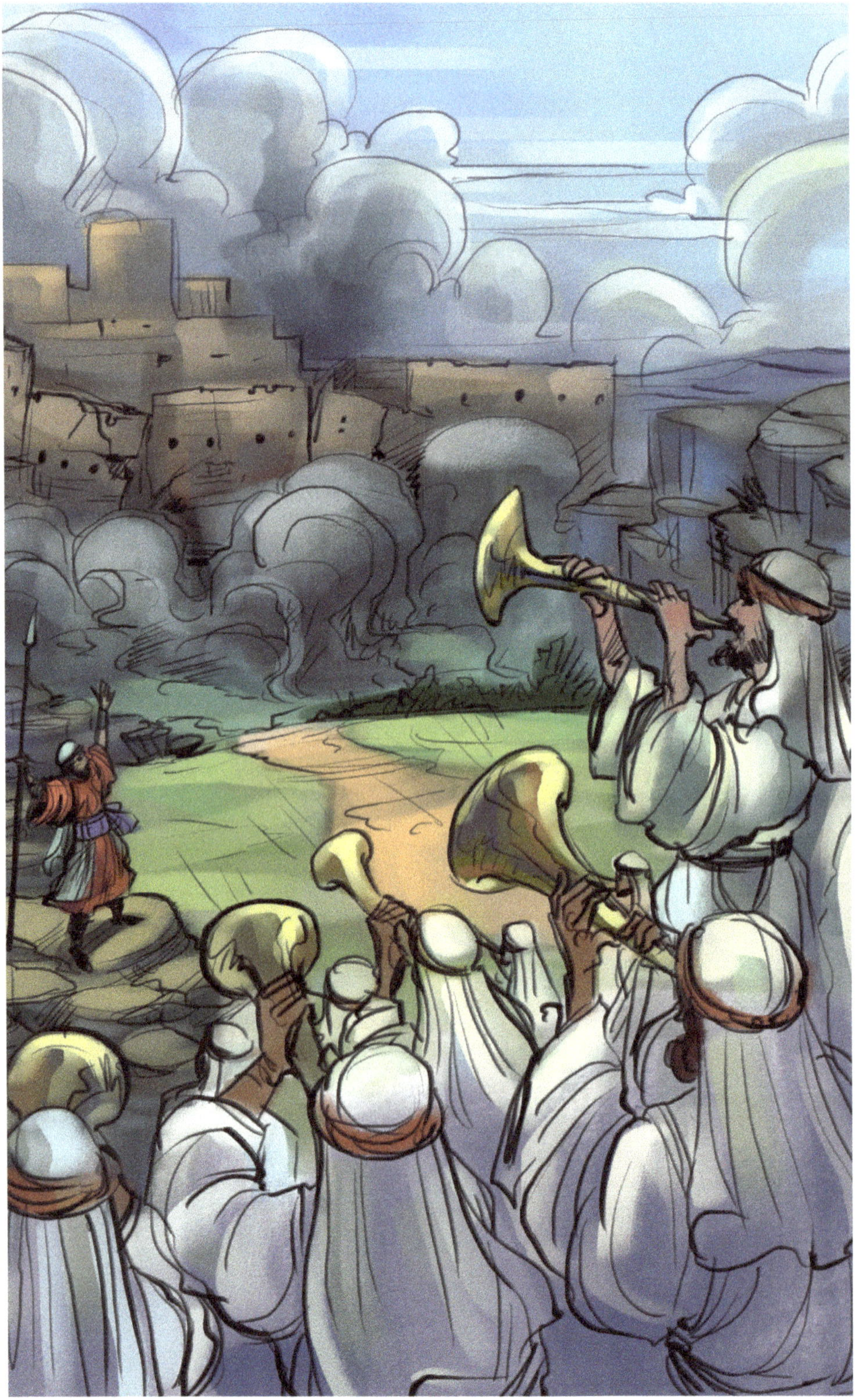

BIBLE ADVENTURE STORIES

When the people in Jericho saw this, they were terrified and ran away. Joshua and his army marched in after them, and they won a great victory for God that day.

This was the first of many victories for Joshua and the Israelites. They trusted in God's plans because God always kept his promises. And the same is true for us today. If we trust God and do what He says, all his promises will come true for us too.

> *"Have faith in God," Jesus answered. "I tell you the truth, if anyone says to this mountain, 'Go, throw yourself into the sea,' and does not doubt in his heart but believes that what he says will happen, it will be done for him. Therefore I tell you, whatever you ask for in prayer, believe that you have received it, and it will be yours.*
>
> **Mark 11:22-24**
> **NIV**

GOD MAKES THE SUN STAND STILL

JOSHUA CHAPTER 10

Joshua and the Israelites were having a lot of victories. This was because God was with them to help them defeat their enemies.

One evil king, named Adoni, was king of Jerusalem at the time. He got really worried that the Israelites would take over his city as well. So he wrote letters to four other evil kings who were friends of his to ask if they would help him fight against the Israelites. The other kings lived near him and they were the kings of a group of people called the Amorites.

So, the other evil kings agreed to join Adoni. When they all came together, their army was huge and had many great warriors.

The first thing they did was go to a town called Gibeon. They attacked it because this town had made peace with Joshua.

The king from Gibeon sent someone to Joshua to ask for help because his army wasn't big enough to defeat the Amorite's bigger army. Also, Joshua promised the Gibeonites that if they were ever in trouble that he and his army would come back and defend them.

Well, Joshua was an honest man and he stood by his promises. So, he and his army came to help the king and people of Gibeon. Joshua called all his soldiers together and they set out for Gibeon.

Joshua's army marched all night so that they could surprise the Amorite army. In the morning, they battled the Amorites and chased them away from Gibeon. God also helped Joshua and his army by throwing large hailstones down from the sky on the enemy soldiers to knock them out. Just imagine giant ice balls falling from the sky and hitting people. OUCH!

But many of the evil Amorite soldiers started running and hiding. It started getting dark, so it made it easy for the Amorite soldiers to hide from Joshua. So, Joshua asked God to do something impossible—he asked

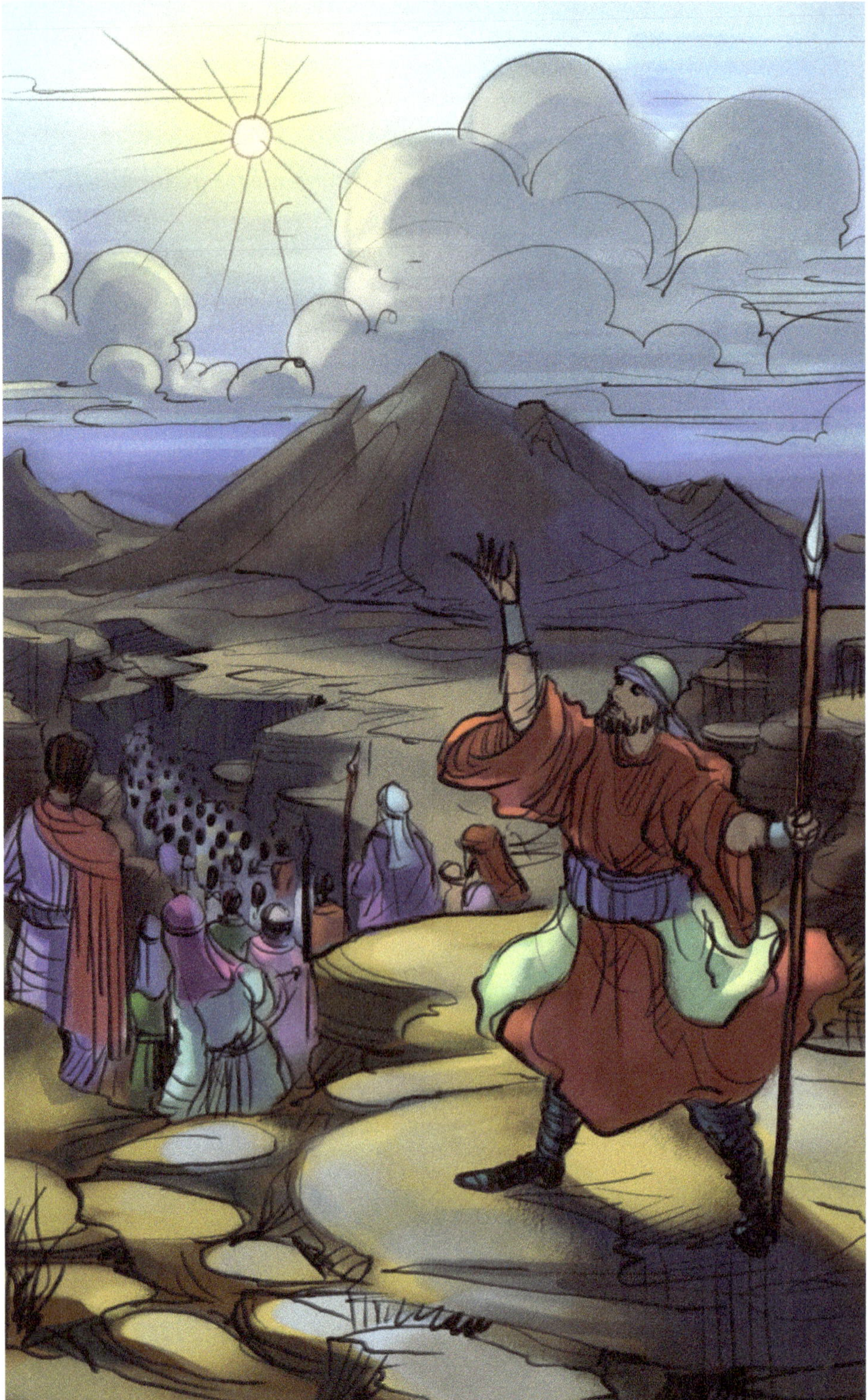

BIBLE ADVENTURE STORIES

God to stop the sun from going down so that he could completely defeat the Amorite army.

And guess what?

God did it! God made the sun stand still.

For a whole day, God made the sun stand still in the sky so that Joshua and his army could chase the evil Amorite soldiers so far away that they would never come back. The Israelites took over the five cities that belonged to the Amorites, and saved the people of Gibeon. It was the only time in the history of the world that God had stopped the sun from going down for an entire day.

God can do even more amazing things than that, because He's that strong and powerful. And God will do amazing things for us, too, if we just ask Him too. Now, He may not make the sun stand still, but if we keep praying He will do more amazing things than we can ever ask or imagine.

> *God can do anything, you know—far more than you could ever imagine or guess or request in your wildest dreams!*
>
> **Ephesians 3:20**
> **MSG**

SAMSON DEFEATS THE PHILISTINES

JUDGES CHAPTER 16

After God freed His people from their enemies, they loved God and followed him for many years. But then God's people forgot about Him again, and stopped obeying Him. They actually started to worship other gods and started doing really evil things. So, like a father, God had to discipline his children so that they could become grateful again. God wanted to make sure that His people would make it to heaven one day.

So, God let other countries come in and rule over the Israelites. And these other countries were not very nice. A group of evil people called the Philistines really treated the Israelites badly, and made their lives very hard.

The Israelites became very sad and grew tired of the way their lives were going. When they got tired of all of their trouble, they cried out to God, and asked God to help them. God felt really bad for them, because even though He disciplined them, He cared about them very much.

So, God decided to raise up a hero to save them.

God sent an angel to a woman who wasn't able to have any kids and he told her that she would finally be able to have a child. The angel told the woman that her son was going to save the Israelites from the evil Philistines.

Now God had special rules that He wanted the boy to follow. But the woman didn't mind because she was so happy to be able to have a son of her own.

When the boy was finally born, his mother named him Samson. God gave Samson a special gift that would help him save God's people from the Philistines. He gave him the gift of super strength.

So Samson grew up and became a powerful man. One day, when the Philistines were bullying the Israelites, Samson went out and saved them by beating up 30 men. Another time, he struck down 1,000 Philistines with the jawbone of a donkey.

Samson had a secret, though, that only he and his parents knew about. The reason he was so strong was because he never cut his hair. Yeah, I know—that sounds crazy. But it was true. You see, one of those special rules the angel told his parents was that he wasn't supposed to ever to get a haircut. That was because Samson's strength was in his hair. As long as Samson obeyed God and never cut his hair, God would help him do all kinds of great feats.

Even though the Philistines were his enemies, Samson liked one of their women. The Philistines knew this, so they used her to trick him into telling her the secret of his super strength. So, while he was asleep one day, the Philistine woman working for the evil Philistines, cut off his hair.

When Samson woke up, he discovered that his hair was cut. So, when the Philistine men attacked him, he was too weak to stop them. Then they tied Samson up and put him in jail. All the Philistines made fun of him now that he was weak, and they made him do silly tricks for them.

Well, guess what happened? Samson's hair started to grow again. So his great strength started to come back.

One day the leaders of the Philistines threw a big party to celebrate defeating Samson and taking him prisoner. This party was held in a big building, called a temple.

The people and all their leaders went to the party and the temple was full. There were so many people that 3,000 men and women climbed on the roof and watched the party from above.

The people all wanted to see Samson perform tricks for them and to make fun of him. "Come on, Samson. Show us how strong you are," they shouted. "I'll bet my kids are stronger than you," they said. They made fun of him because they thought he wasn't strong anymore and laughed at him.

Now the Philistines didn't know that Samson's strength was coming back, but Samson knew. So, while in chains, Samson had someone show him where the two main pillars were that held up the entire temple. He put his left hand on one of the pillars and his right hand on the other.

In a loud voice, he called out to God, "O God, give me all my great strength back just one last time so that I can destroy the evil Philistines!" And with that, he pushed on the pillars with all his strength and they fell over. When that happened, the roof caved in and all the Philistines in the temple were crushed.

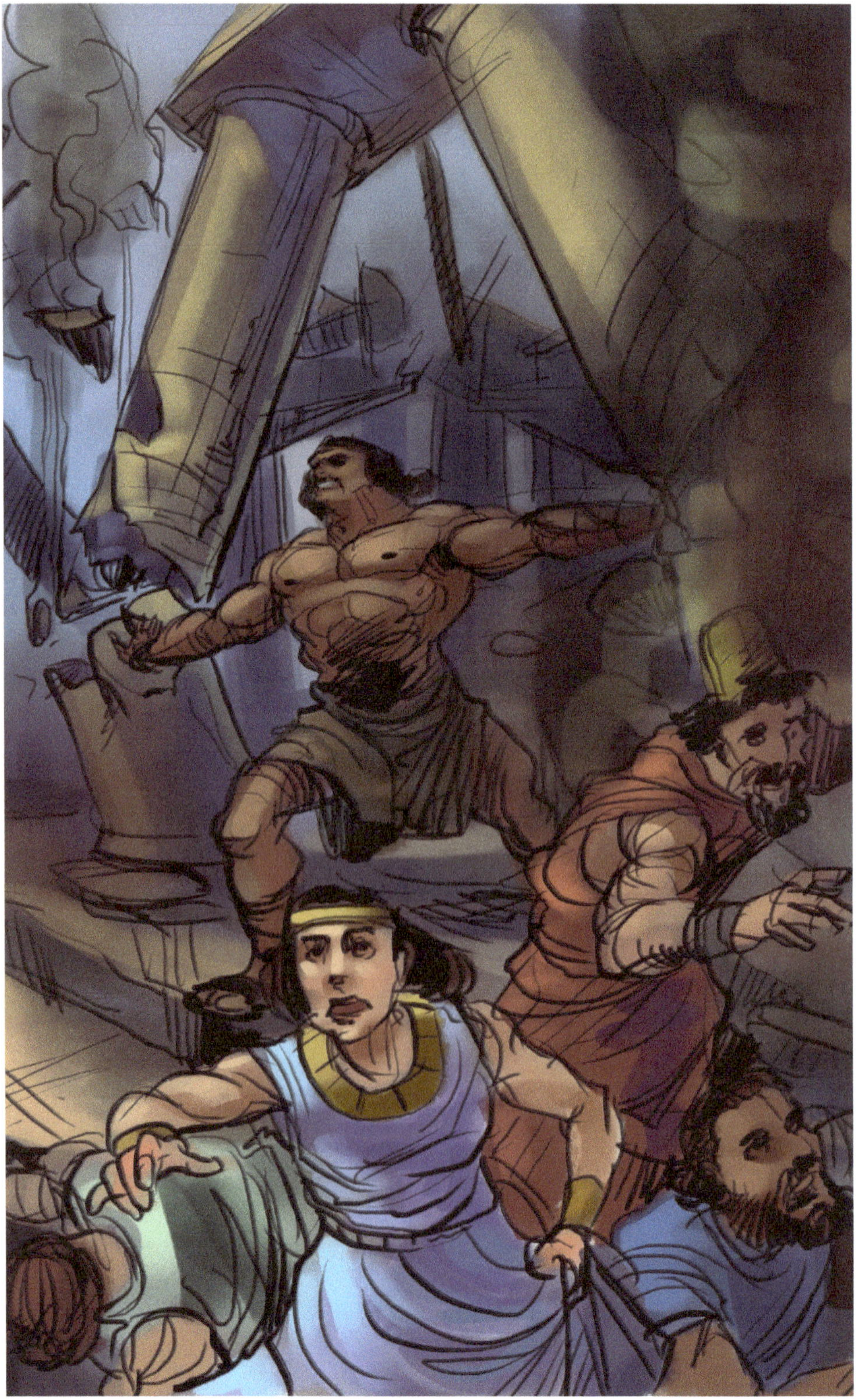

In one super powerful act, God and Samson overcame the Philistines. After that, the Philistines left the Israelites alone for a long time.

I can do everything through [God] who gives me strength.

Philippians 4:13
NIV

DAVID AND GOLIATH

1 SAMUEL CHAPTER 17

Many years later, the Israelites were again at war against the Philistines. One day, the Israelites and the Philistines decided to meet in battle. They both camped on two hills across from each other, with a valley between them.

Now, one of the Philistine soldiers came out of his camp and dared anyone of the Israelites to come fight him. He said, "If any of you can beat me, then we Philistines will become your slaves. But if I beat your man, then you have to become our slaves."

The soldier's name was Goliath.

Twice a day Goliath would come out. But, none of the Israelites took him up on his offer. You see, the Israelites were terrified of him because Goliath was a giant. He was over nine feet tall. If you want to know how tall that is, that's almost as tall as a basketball hoop.

And that's probably taller than the ceiling in your house!

Goliath wore a bronze helmet on his head, a bronze spear on his back, and even bronze boots on his feet. Imagine that—he wore metal boots. All his armor weighed almost 700 pounds, which is almost as heavy as 4 men! Goliath was tough and mean and had been a soldier since he was a boy.

No wonder the Israelites were scared of him. Wouldn't you be afraid if you had to face a giant like that?

Now, there was an Israelite boy named David who was working as a shepherd for his dad, Jesse. He took care of all of Jesse's sheep in the fields. He had eight brothers, and three of his brothers were in the army fighting against the Philistines.

One day Jesse asked David to take some food to David's brothers in the army. David loaded up one of his dad's donkeys with the food and set out for where the two armies were camped. Just as he got there, he heard Goliath's challenge to the Israelites and saw the men shaking in their boots from fear.

He gave the food out just as he'd been told and then asked some of the soldiers, "What will the king do if someone beats this Philistine?" The men said that the king would reward him with all kinds of wealth and even give his own daughter to be the man's wife. He then would become part of the royal family.

David didn't like how Goliath was insulting God and his people, the Israelites. David asked angrily, "Who is this Philistine that he should defy the armies of the living God?"

So David told the soldiers that he would fight Goliath. Some of the soldiers sent this word to Saul, who was the king of the Israelites. Saul was happy that finally someone was brave enough to fight Goliath. He sent for David, thinking he would be a mighty warrior. Instead, David turned out to be a young shepherd boy!

King Saul said, "You can't fight him. You're only a boy and he's been a soldier since he was your age."

David replied, "I've been taking care of my dad's sheep. When a lion or bear attacked the sheep and carried one off, I ran after the wild animal, hit it with my club and saved the sheep. If God saved me from the lion and the bear, He can save me from this giant."

King Saul put his own armor on David and gave him his sword. David tried the armor out but it didn't fit right so he took it off. He was going to fight Goliath with his own weapon—a slingshot. Back then, a slingshot was a short piece of rope with a small leather pouch in the middle that holds a stone. You hold the rope by the ends, twirl it as fast as you can over your head, and let go of one end of the rope, slinging the stone toward the thing you're aiming for.

So, David went to a nearby stream, chose five stones and grabbed his slingshot.

David walked out on the field of battle to fight the Philistine giant. When Goliath saw David, he made fun of him because he saw that David was barely a teenager. "You're going to fight me with sticks and stones?" Goliath growled. "Come here, little boy, and I'll teach you a lesson." Goliath was fully armed with a spear and a sword while David just had a slingshot and some rocks.

But David was not afraid because he was fighting in the name of God. David believed that God would help him even if the situation seemed impossible.

As David and the giant approached each other, David took a stone from his pouch, put it in his slingshot, twirled it over his head and threw it as hard as he could. The stone hit Goliath right on his forehead and he fell to the ground. The stone hit Goliath so hard that it killed him right on the spot.

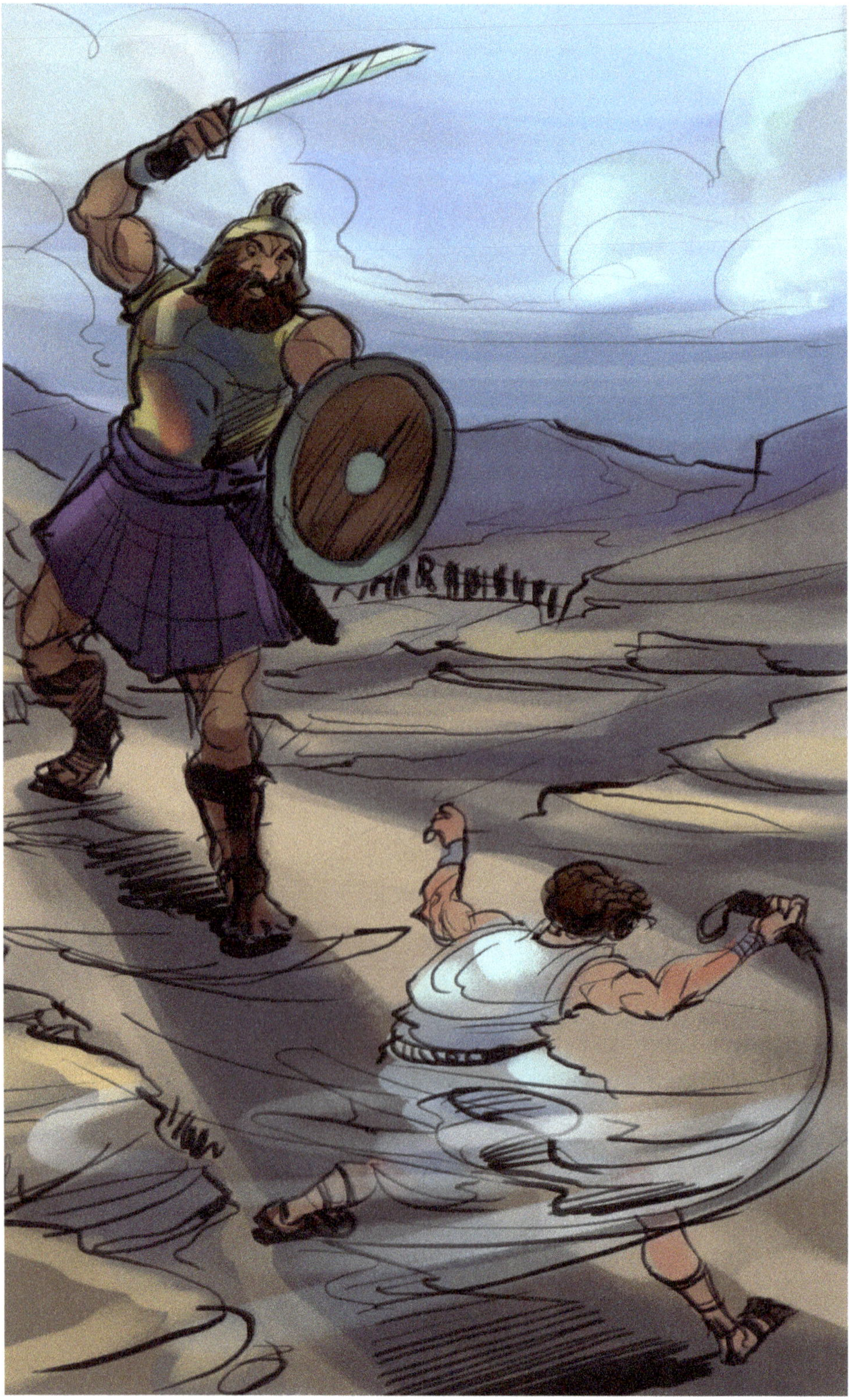

At that moment, the Philistine army became really scared. They thought that if a boy could beat a giant like Goliath, then he could beat the rest of them, too. And when the Israelite army saw what happened, they gave a great shout and ran after the Philistine army. They chased the Philistine army all the way back to the towns they came from.

David became a great hero that day. All the Israelites cheered for him because he was brave and beat Goliath with just a slingshot. Now, if God was able to do that for David, just imagine what he could do for you.

> *"Be strong and courageous, do not be afraid or tremble at them, for the LORD your God is the one who goes with you. He will not fail you or forsake you."*
>
> **Deuteronomy 31:6**
> **NASB**

SOLOMON ASKS FOR WISDOM

1 KINGS CHAPTER 3

King David ruled in Israel for a long time. Finally, he became very old and passed away. He had a son named Solomon who became the next king.

Now, Solomon was a young man when he became king, and leading millions of people is a huge task. There weren't any books written back then like, "How to Be a Great King in Five Simple Steps" or "Being a King Made Easy." It seemed like Solomon would have to figure it out on his own.

Solomon loved God just like his father David had. He lived in a city named Jerusalem, which is where David had lived, too. One day Solomon went to a town a few miles away to be part of a celebration for God. And while he was at the celebration, God appeared to Solomon in a dream.

In Solomon's dream, God appeared to him and just asked him one question. He said, "Solomon, what do you want most in your life? Tell me what it is and I'll do it for you."

Now that's interesting. If God asked you the same question, what would you have asked for? Lots of kids would probably ask for a new toy like a video game or a doll. Or, they might ask to go on a fun vacation to Disneyland. They even might ask for a pony or some cool basketball shoes.

But do you know what Solomon asked for? Solomon asked God for wisdom. Wisdom means knowing how to make the best choices, so that you can please God and help others. Solomon knew he was too young to lead the people of Israel, so he asked God to give him wisdom so he could be the best king he could be.

God was so happy that Solomon asked for wisdom that He said, "Well done, Solomon! I'll grant you your wish and make you very wise. In fact, I'm going to make you the wisest person that ever lived. You could have asked to be really famous or rich. Those things are ok, too, but you asked for the best thing. So you know what, Solomon? Not only am I going to make you wise, I'm also going to make you rich and famous as well.

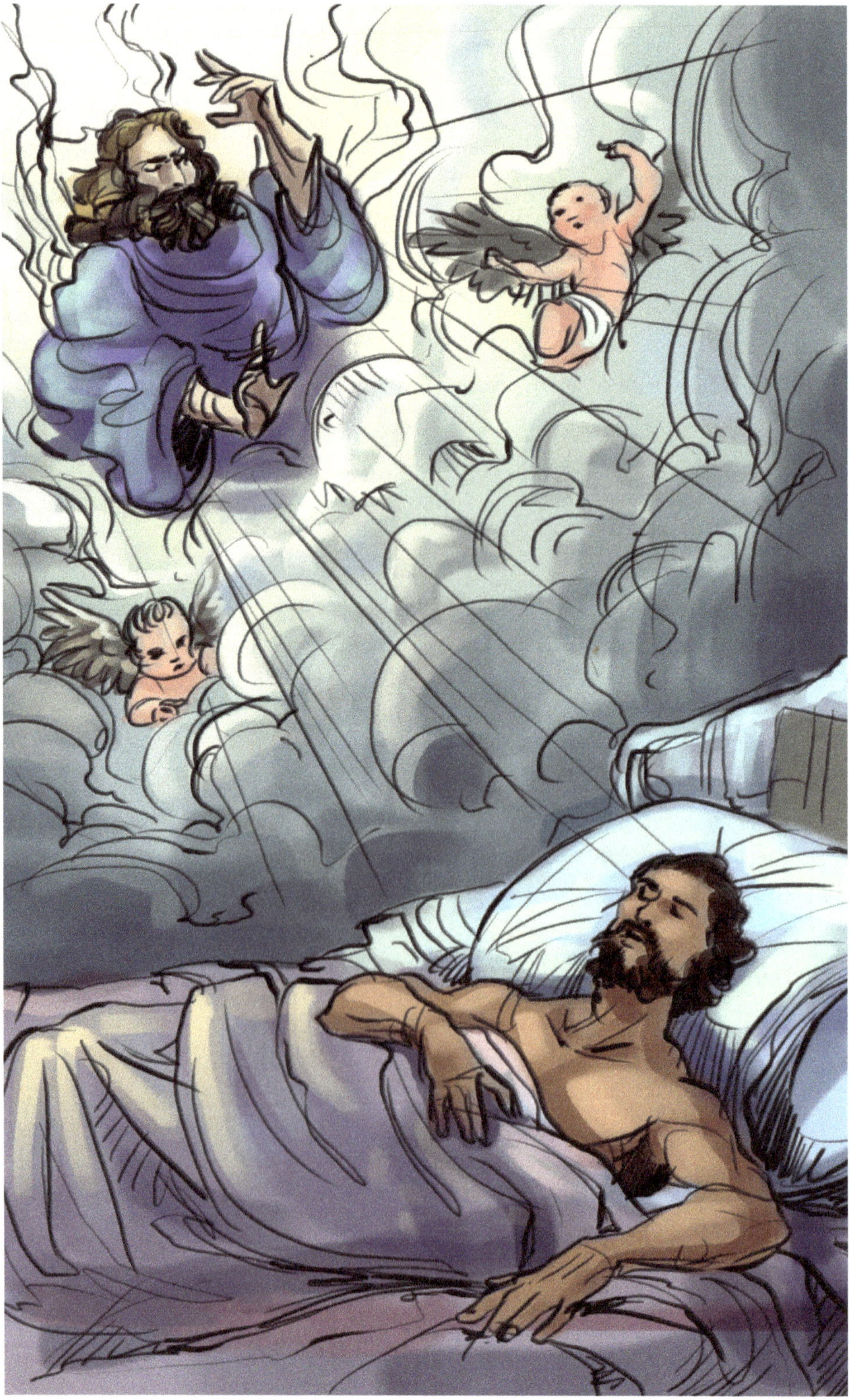

Everyone in Israel will look up to you and people will come from faraway lands to learn from you. Just be sure to believe in Me and do what I ask, and everything will go well for you."

When Solomon woke up, he knew that he'd been dreaming. But he also believed in his heart that he'd really talked with God and that God would do what He promised.

In the course of time, God gave Solomon great wisdom. Solomon was such a wise king, he took really good care of the Israelites. God also helped him become rich, and he was held in honor by everyone who came to see him. The history books tell us that Solomon was the greatest king who ever lived.

God gives us wisdom today through his word, the Bible. And like Solomon, if we follow what He says in the Bible, great things can happen for us, too.

> *But if any of you lacks wisdom, let him ask of God, who gives to all generously and without reproach, and it will be given to him.*
>
> **James 1:5**
> **NASB**

ELIJAH AND THE FALSE PROPHETS

1 KINGS CHAPTER 18

Elijah was a great prophet who lived long ago. A prophet is a messenger of God, someone who speaks to people in God's place, like a teacher. A prophet was a very important person since God used the prophets to teach his people the truth. So, God would share his thoughts with Elijah, and then Elijah would tell the Israelites what God wanted them to know.

In those days, there was a very bad king named Ahab. In fact, the Bible says he was the most evil king of all time in Israel. One of the reasons he was so bad was because he taught God's people not to do what God said but to worship false gods. As a matter of fact, Ahab had 450 false prophets, who taught the people how to worship false gods, instead of how to follow the real God. Since there were so many more of the false prophets and only

BIBLE ADVENTURE STORIES

one real prophet, Elijah, the Israelites believed what the false prophets were teaching.

Now, God sent Elijah to see King Ahab to tell him to stop doing evil. Elijah told the king he was making trouble for the people by letting the false prophets tell lies. King Ahab didn't listen to him or believe him. So Elijah came up with a test to show Ahab and the people of Israel who the real God is, and to show the Israelites who they should follow.

Elijah told Ahab to call together all the false prophets in all of Israel and to meet him at the top of Mount Carmel, where the test would take place. Ahab sent messengers to go through the entire country and had all of the false prophets come to Mount Carmel.

When Ahab and all his prophets were together, Elijah said, "Here's the test. We'll both build a table of stones, called an altar. Then we'll get a pile of wood and put it on the altar. Finally, we'll each bring a big piece of raw meat and put it on the pile of wood. You call on the name of your god, and I will call on God Almighty. The god who answers with fire is the one true God."

Many of the people of Israel were there to watch what happened so that they, too, could find out which one was the real God.

So, the false prophets went first. All morning long they danced and shouted to their false gods to send fire from the sky and burn up their piece of meat. But nothing happened. Elijah started to make fun of them. He said, "Shout louder. Maybe your god is busy running errands, or on a trip. He might be asleep, and you may have to wake him up."

So the false prophets shouted louder and danced harder all afternoon. They cut themselves with their swords, which was also their way of trying to get their god's attention. But, by now it was almost dark and still nothing happened. No one had answered or even noticed.

Now it was Elijah's turn. First he dug a ditch around his altar. He called some of the Israelites who were watching to get four huge water jars and pour water all over the raw meat, the wood, and the stones, which they did. He told them to do it again. Then he told them to do it a third time. There was so much water that it ran off the altar and filled up the whole ditch. Elijah wanted to make sure that everyone knew it would take a miracle for the wood that was soaking wet to catch fire.

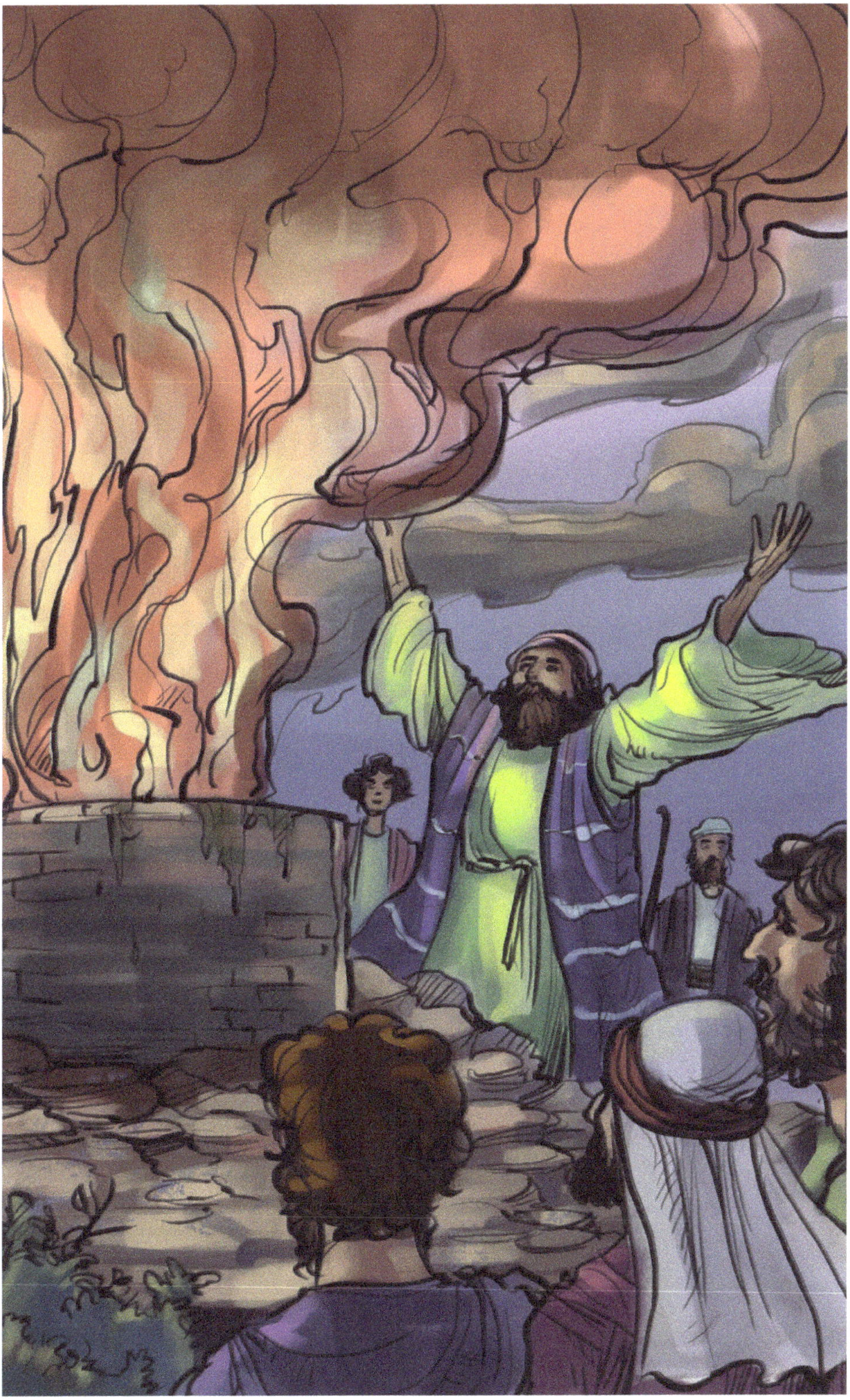

Elijah called out in a loud voice, "O God of Israel, answer me with fire so that all the people will know that You alone are the true God and that they should follow what You say."

Suddenly, fire fell from the sky. It was so hot that it burned up the wood, the meat, the stones, the water in the ditch, and even the ground, which turned black.

The people saw this and shouted, "The God of Elijah is the true God! Let's believe in him and do what He says."

That's how God proved that Elijah was a true prophet and that He is the true God. God performed a miracle that only the real God could do. So, all of the people decided to believe in the one true God, who is awesome and powerful.

> *...The prayer of a righteous man is powerful and effective.*
>
> **James 5:16**
> **NIV**

ESTHER SAVES HER PEOPLE

ESTHER CHAPTERS 3-9

One time, there was a Jewish girl named Esther that lived in the city of Susa, which was the capital city of Persia. A Jew is another name for an Israelite, one of God's people.

Esther had lost her parents when she was still young. But, she had an older cousin, named Mordecai, who adopted her and treated her as if she was his own daughter.

During that time, Xerxes, the king of Persia, held a beauty contest to find the prettiest girl in the kingdom. Many beautiful women went to Susa to take part but Esther was the most beautiful of them all. She was also very nice and lots of people liked her. Mordecai told her not to tell anyone that she was a Jew because he was afraid that she wouldn't be treated well if other people knew. The people of that country didn't like the Jews very much so it was probably better for Mordecai and Esther to keep that secret to themselves.

King Xerxes liked Esther more than all the other women in the contest and he made her his queen. She got to wear a crown and King Xerxes threw a big party for her. He even made it into a special holiday for everyone in the kingdom. Queen Esther must have felt very proud and honored.

In spite of all this good luck, there was a bad man named Haman who hated the Jews. He also lived in Susa, where Mordecai and Esther lived. And to make matters worse, he was the king's best friend.

King Xerxes didn't know how much Haman didn't like the Jews. But, Haman came up with a plan to trick the king into getting rid of the Jews. He told the king, "The Jews don't honor you or obey your laws. You should get rid of them before they cause you and the kingdom trouble."

That was a lie but the king fell for it.

"What do you want to do?" King Xerxes asked.

"I think you should make a law that says on a certain day, we should get rid of all the Jews in the entire kingdom,"

Haman replied. So the king agreed. The rule was written down and sent to all parts of the kingdom.

When Mordecai heard about this unfair law, he was scared and sent a message to Queen Esther. He told her about it and asked her to talk to the king. Maybe she could change his mind and get him to take the law back.

Queen Esther wrote back to Mordecai, saying "I can't just show up in front of the king. He has to ask me to see him. The law says that if I see him without getting permission, I could be in big trouble."

Mordecai sent her another note and said, "These are your people and they need your help. Besides, if the king finds out that you're a Jew, you and your family won't be saved either. Maybe God let you become queen for this very reason—so that you can help save the lives of all the Jews living in this land."

Esther was stuck. Should she keep quiet and try to save only herself and her family? Or should she risk her life to see if she can help her people?

But Esther was brave and decided to see the king. She sent a note to Mordecai, asking him and all the Jews to pray to God to protect her. So, for three days, Esther and the Jews prayed that God would help King Xerxes listen to Esther's request, and save the Jews in the land.

So, Queen Esther went to the room where King Xerxes sat on his throne. When she walked in, he was there in deep thought. Esther took a deep breath and walked toward the king. When he saw her, he waved his staff, letting her know she could come forward.

"What can I do for you, my queen?" King Xerxes asked.

"I'd like to throw a party for you," Esther replied. "And at the party, I want to ask you a very special request. Also, I'd like to invite your friend, Haman, as well."

"Very well," said the king. "We'll both be there."

So Queen Esther got everything ready for the party. Both the king and Haman came. They all ate and had a great time. Then after dinner, King Xerxes asked Esther, "Now, what was it you wanted to ask me about?"

Esther reminded him about the rule to get rid of all the Jews in the kingdom. She bravely shared that she was a Jew herself. She asked the king to help protect her and the Jews on the day when people were planning to get rid of the Jews.

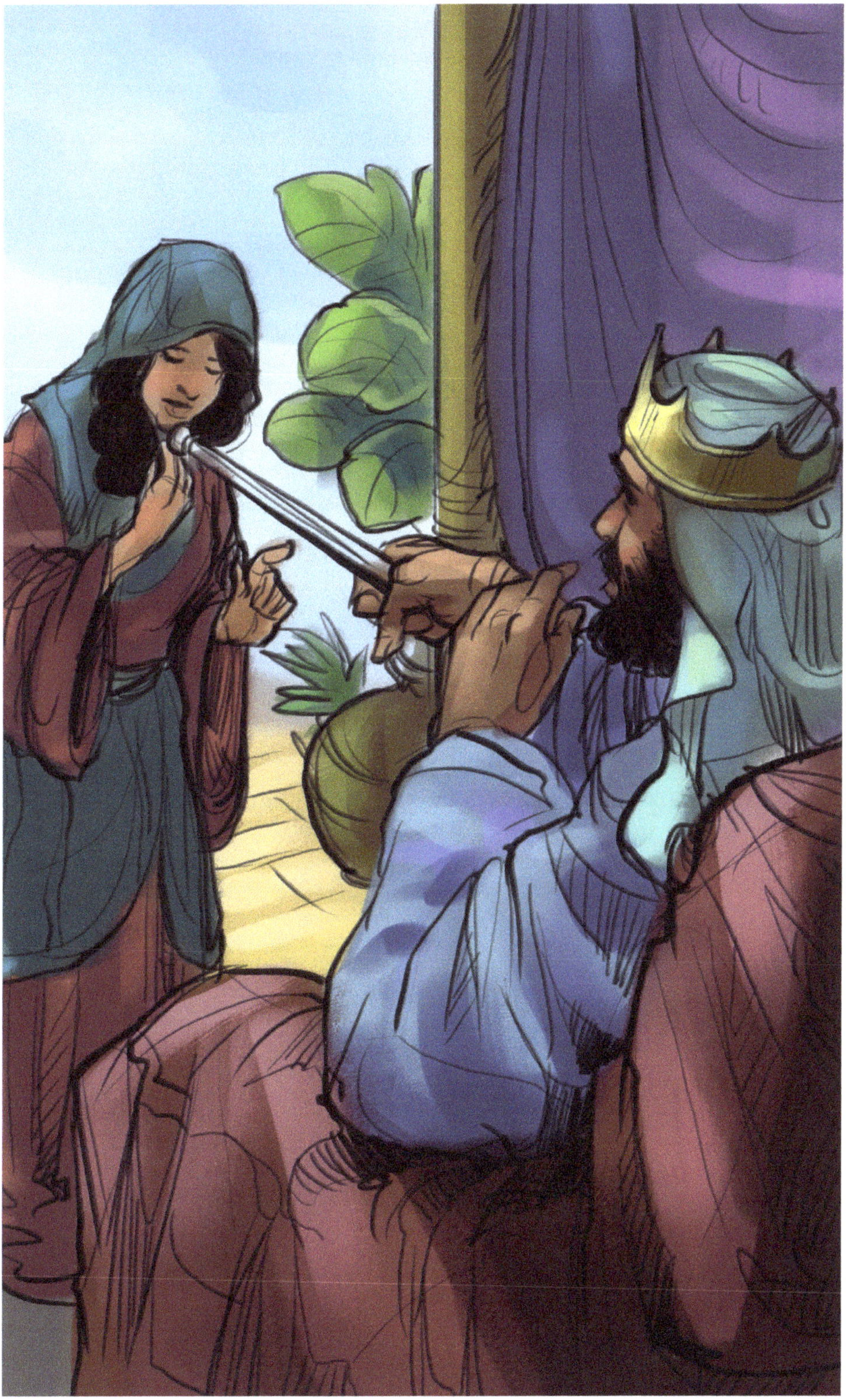

At once, King Xerxes knew that he had made a mistake. "Whose idea was it to come up with such a law?" he asked angrily.

"It was Haman's idea," the queen answered.

Haman knew he was in big trouble. King Xerxes was so mad he had to leave the room to calm down. Haman rushed over to Queen Esther to try to talk his way out his situation. Just then, the king came back and thought Haman was attacking Esther. So he had Haman arrested and Haman was never allowed to enter the king's presence again.

The king couldn't take back the first law he made so he wrote another law allowing the Jews to defend themselves if anyone tried to hurt them. He sent the order to all the parts of his kingdom. So, when the day came when the Jews were going to be attacked, the Jews were able to fight back. God was with them and he helped them defeat their enemies.

Because she loved God and her people, Esther was courageous and helped save all the Jews in her country. She also showed that women can be strong, and that God uses them in special ways, too.

BIBLE ADVENTURE STORIES

Charm can mislead and beauty soon fades. The woman to be admired and praised is the woman who [loves] God.

Proverbs 31:30
MSG

JOB PROVES HIS WORTH

JOB CHAPTERS 1-2, 42

A long time ago in a land called Uz was a man named Job (his name rhymes with 'robe'.) He believed in God and always obeyed him.

Job had seven sons and three daughters. Job was also very rich, because he owned thousands of animals like sheep and camels. He was famous and many people looked up to him because he was a kind and good man.

One day, all the angels in heaven came to report to God. Now, do you know what an angel is? Angels are very powerful beings who live in heaven with God and serve God as his helpers.

Now, a really bad angel, called Satan, came to see God, too. He was a bad angel because he thought he was better than God, and he was jealous of God. So God kicked him out of heaven.

When Satan came and presented himself before God, God asked him, "Where have you come from?"

"I've been traveling all over the world checking out these people you created," Satan told him.

"Have you seen my friend, Job?" God asked. "He's kind and good and helps others because he follows me."

"That's only because you protect him," Satan said. "If you stop helping him, I bet that he won't believe in you anymore or do what you want him to."

"Ok. Go ahead and do everything you want to him, but you can't hurt his body," God replied. "And after you have done these things, you will see how faithful Job will be."

So Satan went out to attack Job. He sent some thieves to steal a lot of Job's animals and to capture some of Job's servants. Then Satan sent fire from the sky and burned up all of Job's fields and sheep. Finally, Job's kids were having a party at one of their houses when Satan caused a sudden, huge wind to knock down their house. So, in just a few hours, everything Job had was gone!

Imagine what it'd be like if everything that you loved and cared for was taken away in just a few hours. That would be the scariest, saddest thing ever, wouldn't it? That must have been how Job felt.

But do you know what Job did? As sad as he was, Job still trusted God and believed that God was good to him. So Job just thanked God for loving him and for being his friend.

Then, on another day, the angels stood before God again, and Satan came, too.

"Did you see my friend, Job?" God asked. "You did all those bad things to him and he still follows me."

"Yeah," replied Satan. "But if you allow me to hurt his body, I'll bet he won't believe in you after that."

"Ok," God said. "I'll let you hurt his body, but you can't kill him."

Well, after everything else he'd done to him, Satan caused painful sores to break out on Job, from the top of his head to the bottom of his feet. He was in so much pain, all he could do was sit on the ground. Job's wife came to him and said, "Why do you still believe in God? Look at all the bad things that have happened to you."

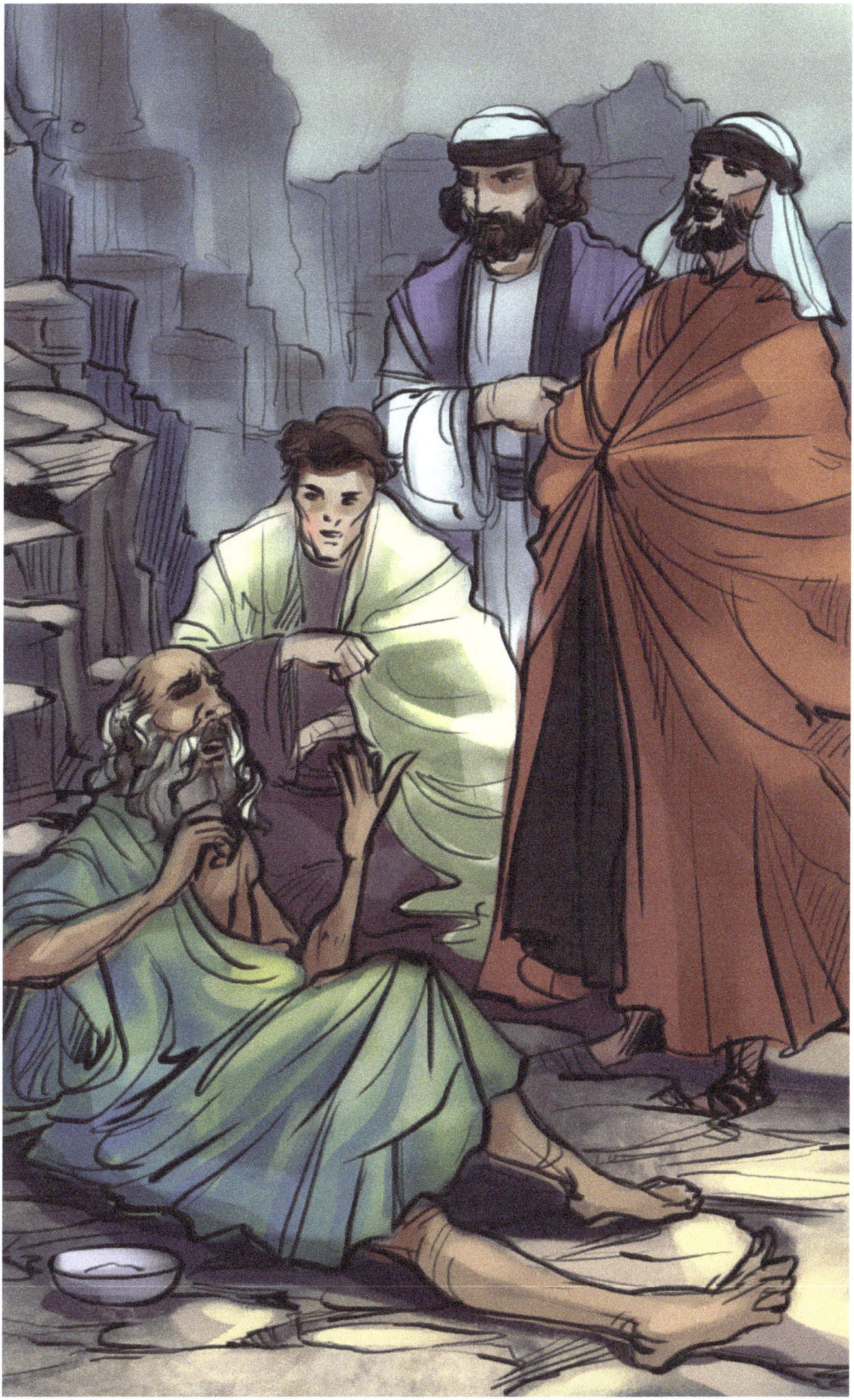

"You're wrong," Job told his wife. "Should we only accept the good things God does for us and not trouble? Good and bad things happen to everyone. I'd still rather believe in God than live without him."

Now that's incredible! Job had great faith, which meant that he believed that God was good even when bad things happened. We can have faith like Job's if we believe that God always loves us and cares for us; even in times of trouble.

But that's not the end of the story! God was so happy that Job was faithful to him during these tough times, that after all of Job's trials God gave Job twice as much as he had before! Job had seven more sons and three more daughters. He had twice as many helpers and more animals than you can count.

It goes to show you that God will reward us if we believe in Him and trust Him, no matter how tough things get.

> *After you have suffered for a little while, the God of all grace, who called you to His eternal glory in Christ, will Himself perfect, confirm, strengthen and establish you.*
>
> **1 Peter 5:10-11**
> **NASB**

DANIEL AND HIS FRIENDS

DANIEL CHAPTER 3

A new nation called the Babylonians became powerful and took over the nation of Israel. Their leader was a man named King Nebuchadnezzar (we'll call him King Neb for short.) He lived in a city called Babylon.

Now, the city of Babylon was really big and King Neb needed many wise men to help run it. He looked for the wisest men in the land he could find to come help him. He found four very wise Israelite men in Babylon, and he brought them to his palace to help run the city of Babylon as well. Their names were Daniel, Shadrach, Meshach and Abednego (we'll just call Daniel's friends, Shad, Shack and Abe for short.) They were the wisest of the wise men and Daniel was smartest of them all. So King Neb put Daniel and his three friends in charge of the city.

The king believed in a god that was different than the God of the Israelites. He built a statue of this other god that was 90 feet tall and made of gold. He had it set up in a big field in Babylon, and it could be seen from many miles away. He wanted everyone to bow down to the statue, so that they could pay honor to his god, too. So, at certain times during the day, he would have all kinds of music played. When the people heard the music, they were supposed to stop what they were doing, go to the field and bow down to the statue.

If you think about it, it seems kind of silly to bow down to a statue that someone made out of metal. How can an object that someone built with his hands help anybody? That would be like asking one of your stuffed animals to help you do better in school, or help you deal with a school bully. If you did that, your friends would think you were crazy. But when you're a king, like King Neb, you get to order people to do silly things like that.

Daniel, Shad, Shack and Abe only believed in the real God, who is God of everything and the true King of the Universe. One day, when Daniel's friends, Shad, Shack, and Abe were working together, the music played, but they didn't go to the field to worship the statue. They believed that if they bowed down to a false god they would dishonor the true God. So, they just kept on working.

Some evil men in the city saw this and went to the king to tell on Shad, Shack and Abe because they were jealous of them. So the king called them to see him.

"What's this story I've heard that you won't bow down and worship my god?" King Neb asked.

"That's right," Shad, Shack and Abe replied. "We believe in the real God and not in your statue."

"If you don't do what I ask, I'll have you burned up in a fire," King Neb added.

"That's fine with us," the three said. "Our God can save us if He wants to, but even if He doesn't, we're still not going to bow down to your statue."

That made the king really mad! He was so mad that he had them thrown into a giant oven. He made the fire in the oven seven times hotter than usual. Then he had his strongest men tie up Shad, Shack, and Abe with thick ropes and throw them into the fire.

After a while, the king went to check on Shad, Shack and Abe. When he looked into the giant oven he saw that Shad, Shack and Abe were still alive, and the fire was not even burning them! Now only that, he saw that there was a fourth man in the fire and he was shining

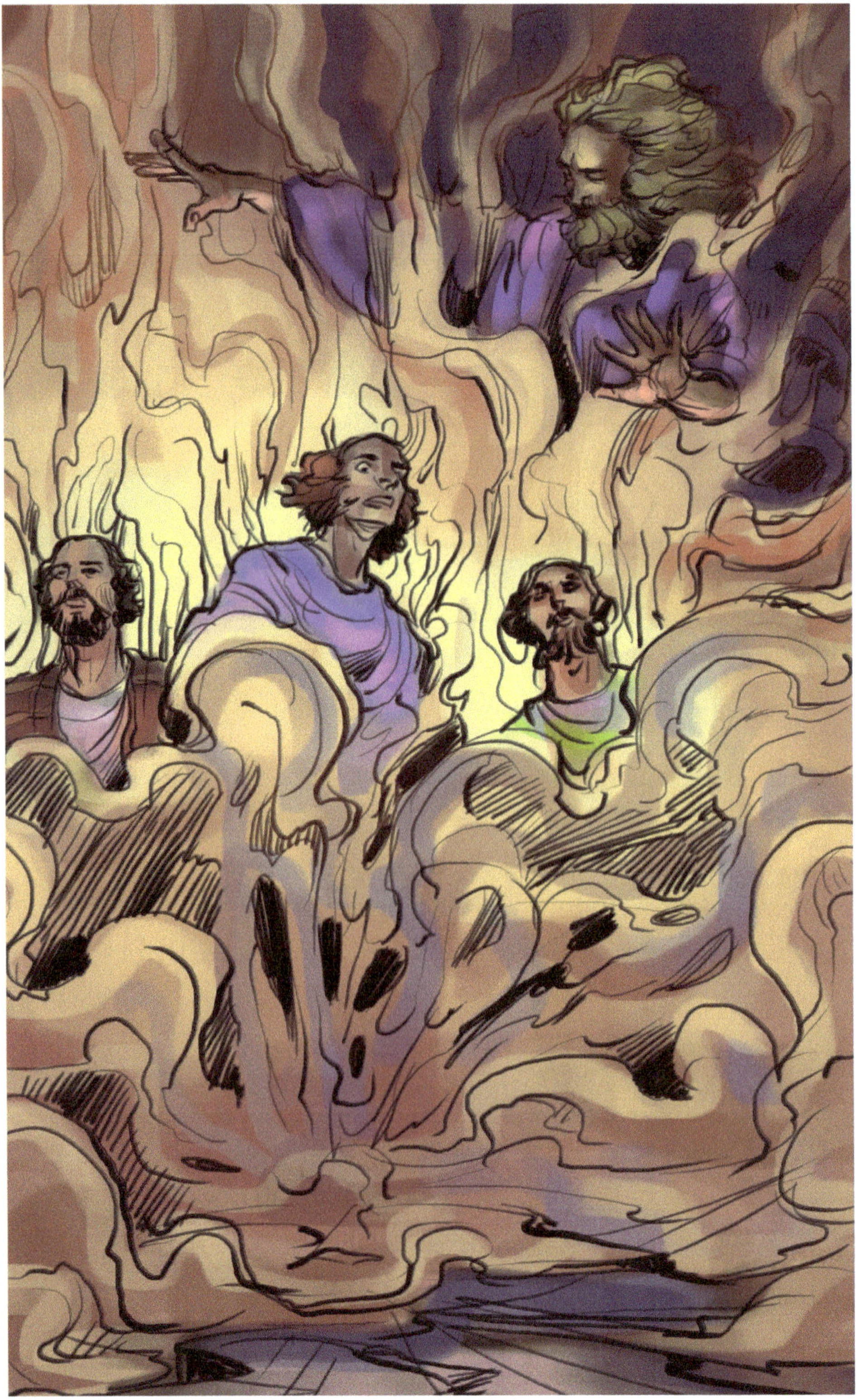

brightly, like an angel. King Neb didn't know what to think about what he saw so he called out to the three men, "Shad, Shack and Abe, come out at once!"

The three men stepped out of the fire. They weren't burned at all, and they didn't even smell like smoke! Then King Neb said, "Only the real God of Shad, Shack and Abe could have saved them from this fire. They chose to obey their God rather than me and He helped them. From this time forward, I'm making a law that says if anyone says anything bad about their God, that person will be thrown into a an oven and their house will be knocked down."

Then the king gave even more power and honor to Shad, Shack and Abe than they had before.

It's good to trust in God when we're faced with doing something that's hard for us. Because God will always help us in our time of need.

> *Let us then approach [God's] throne of grace with confidence, [through prayer], so that we may receive mercy and find grace to help us in our time of need.*
> **Hebrews 4:16**
> **NIV**

DANIEL IN THE LIONS' DEN

DANIEL CHAPTER 6

Years later, Daniel also served another man, Darius, the king of the Persians and the Medes. King Darius also had very wise men that helped him run his kingdom. Those men were led by three special men who were wiser than everyone else. Those three men reported only to the king; and one of those men was Daniel.

Now, because Daniel was so good at his job, King Darius decided to make him head over all the others who ran the kingdom. This made the other men jealous, so they looked for a way to get Daniel in trouble. But Daniel was honest and truthful, which is another reason why the king liked him so much.

"There must be some other way we can get Daniel in trouble," they said. "It will have to be something about him and his God." So they came up with a plan to get Daniel in trouble by testing his faith in God.

BIBLE ADVENTURE STORIES

In those days, people who didn't believe in the God of the Israelites prayed to other gods or even to the king, because he was their leader. To pray means to talk to God and to tell him how you feel or to ask him for help with your problems. Daniel prayed to God a lot, so God answered his prayers and gave him success in everything he did.

The evil men who were jealous of Daniel went to King Darius and said, "O great King Darius! Everyone in the kingdom should look up to you for your power and greatness. Make a law so that all the people should pray only to you or to one of your gods and to no one else. If anyone does pray to another God but you, they should be thrown into the lion's den." A lion's den is a big place where a lot of lions live. This idea pleased the king, so he had the law written down and all the people were told about it.

Daniel heard about the new law, too. It meant that if he kept praying to God, he would be thrown into the lion's den. Lions are always hungry and Daniel knew they would eat him if he was thrown into their den. He must have been really scared. So he had to make a choice: Should he keep praying to God or should he do what the law said?

Daniel chose to do the right thing and kept praying to God, who helped him in many ways. Three times a day he got down on his knees and spoke to God. During one of those times, some of the bad men caught him and told the king about it. At that moment, King Darius saw that those other men had tricked him into making a law that would get Daniel in trouble, and he was mad! But because he had made the law, he had to follow it or else no one would follow any rule he made. So he had Daniel taken to the lion's den and thrown in. The king really cared about Daniel and he called out to him, "Daniel, may your God who you pray to keep you safe tonight!"

The king was so upset that he couldn't eat or sleep all night. In the morning, when the sun was just coming up, he hurried to the lion's den to see what happened. "Daniel, are you alive?" he cried out.

"Yes, O king," Daniel said. "The God that I serve sent an angel to shut the mouths of the lions so that they wouldn't eat me."

The king was super happy! He had Daniel pulled out of the lion's den and they hugged each other.

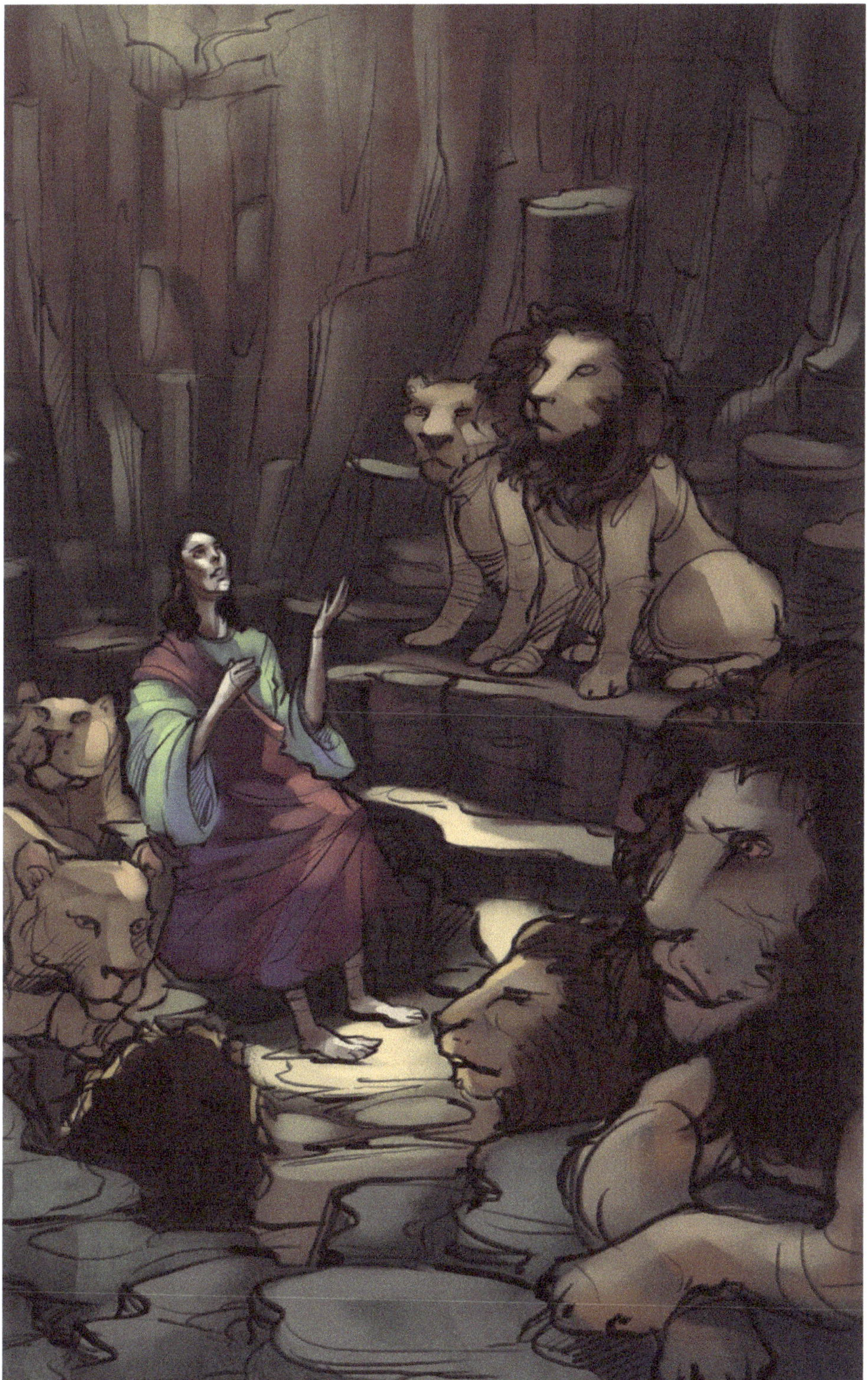

Then King Darius made another new rule, which said: "Everyone in my kingdom should pray to Daniel's God, who is the one true God. He does miracles and great things for all people. He rules over all the world and He rescued Daniel from the lion's den."

Not only did God rescue Daniel, but He continued to help him be a good helper to King Darius and gave him success in everything he did.

> *As the mountains surround Jerusalem, So the LORD [protects] His people...forever*
>
> **Psalms 125:2**
> **NASB**

JONAH AND THE BIG FISH

JONAH CHAPTER 1-3

Jonah was a believer in God who lived in Israel. One day, God asked Jonah to go to a city in a land far away, called Nineveh, and help the people there. He was to tell the people of Nineveh that they should stop doing bad things and believe in God, too.

Jonah thought about it. *"Man, that city is really far away. It's going to take me a couple of months to get there. Robbers may attack me and take all my stuff. I might run out of food and die on the way there. And once I get there, the people may not like what I say to them and they might really hurt me!"*

Jonah thought about it some more—and then he took off in the opposite direction! He got on a boat that was going the opposite direction of where God told him to go. He thought he could run away from God.

But God sees everything and He saw Jonah on the boat trying to run away. So, God sent a storm on the sea to get his attention. The wind blew really hard and the waves got high and tossed the boat around as if it was a stick in the water.

All the sailors on the boat were super scared and they cried out to their gods for help. But Jonah went down inside the boat and fell asleep. I don't know how could he sleep in the middle of a huge storm, but he did. The sailors looked around for Jonah because he wasn't on the deck of the boat with them. After a while, they found him down in the middle of the boat, asleep.

"How can you sleep at a time like this?" they asked. "Why aren't you calling on your god? Who are you? What have you done?"

"I serve the one true God," Jonah replied. "And I'm running away from Him because He asked me to do something I don't want to do," he added. "But if you throw me off the boat, the storm will stop."

The men didn't want to do that because they knew Jonah would drown. They tried even harder to row to shore but the wind and the waves grew wilder and the boat was about to sink. Finally, the sailors asked God to forgive them if Jonah drowned—and then they threw him off the boat.

Splash! Jonah hit the water and started to sink. At that moment, God made a giant fish come up from the sea and swallow Jonah. All of a sudden, the storm stopped and the water became calm. When the sailors saw this, they believed in the God of Jonah because He had the power to make the storm go away.

Jonah was in the belly of the fish for three days. It smelled really bad, like rotten eggs, old fish and sour milk mixed together. Yuck! Jonah was also soaking wet. And because he didn't have anything to eat inside the fish, he was hungry.

Jonah knew what he had to do. So, he finally prayed to God for help. Jonah said, "God, you have all the power. I know you can hear me inside this big fish and I'm really sorry I ran away. I promise to do what you asked me to if you'll get me out of here."

God listened to Jonah and He told the fish to take Jonah to shore, where he spit him out onto dry land. Then Jonah went to Nineveh and he told everyone there that they needed to believe in God and become good people. And you know what? The people did what he said! They stopped doing the bad things they were doing and started praying to God, just like Jonah.

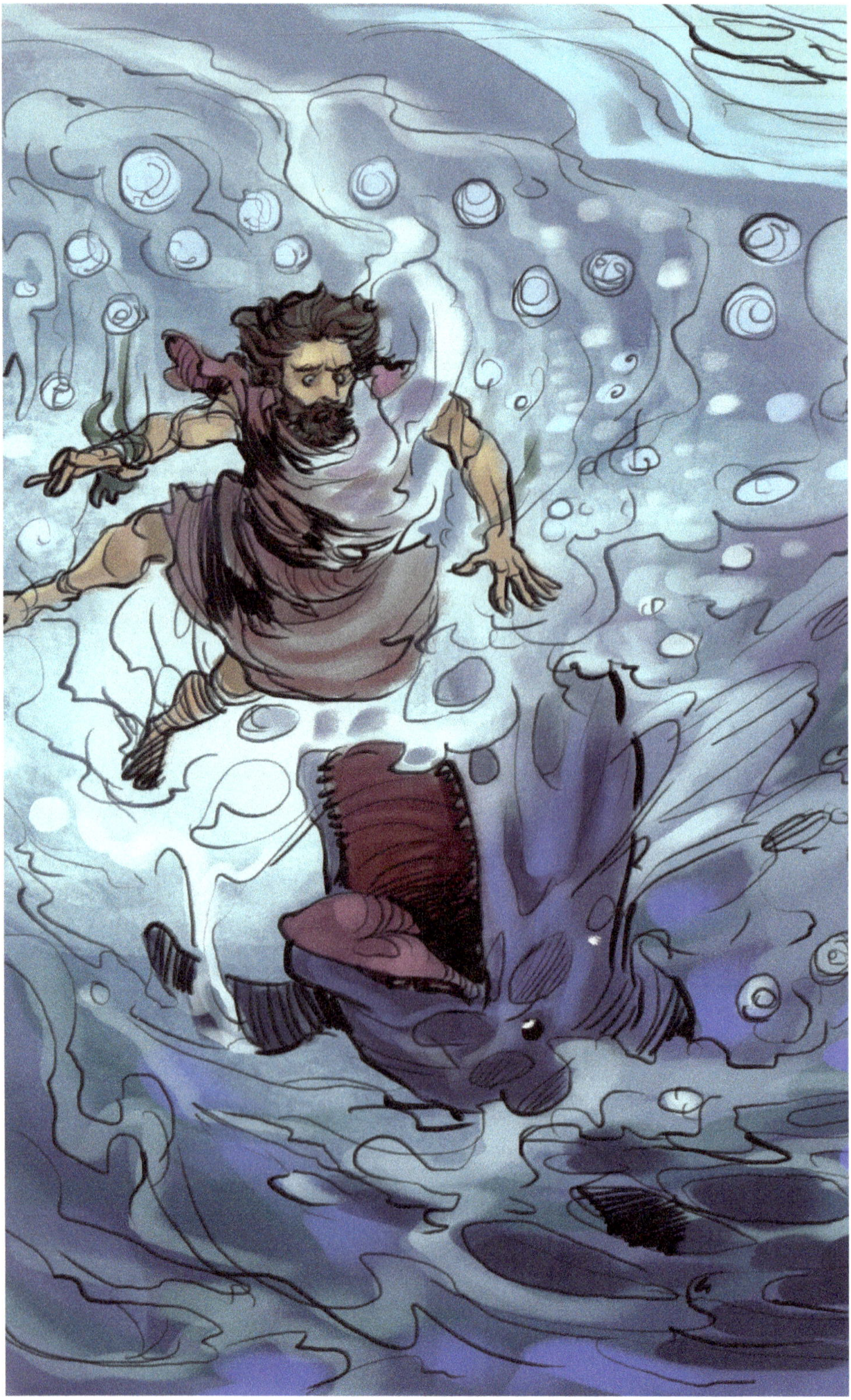

BIBLE ADVENTURE STORIES

So, like Jonah and the Ninevites, no matter how much we may disobey God in our life, it is never too late to ask God for help. We always have the choice to turn back to God, and choose to love Him and obey Him again in our lives

> *"Now it's time to change your ways! Turn to face God so he can wipe away your sins, [and] pour out showers of blessing to refresh you…"*
>
> **Acts 3:18-19**
> **MSG**

JESUS IS BORN

MATTHEW CHAPTERS 1-2, LUKE CHAPTERS 1-2

Jesus is the most important person who ever lived. He's special because He was the son of God and He was born so that we could get to know God better and have a relationship with Him. This is the story of how Jesus came into the world.

There was once a Jewish girl named Mary. She was a very good person, so God chose her to be the mother of Jesus.

One day God sent an angel, called Gabriel, to see her. Gabriel told Mary that God thought very highly of her and that He wanted her to be Jesus' mom. He also said that Jesus would be a powerful man and that He would bring freedom to all the people on earth if they believed in God.

Mary was blown away! She was just a poor girl who lived with her parents. She didn't really understand what Gabriel told her. But Mary trusted God, and so she knew that what Gabriel said was true.

Joseph was Mary's husband, and Jesus' dad on earth. An angel also appeared to Joseph in a dream. He told Joseph that Jesus was going to be special and to not be afraid of things that were going to happen. Joseph was a good man who believed in God, so he trusted the angel too.

Just before Jesus was born, the king who ruled over Israel wanted to count everyone for his records. All the people had to sign up in the town where their family was from. Joseph had come from Bethlehem, so that's where he and Mary had to go. It wasn't too far away but it wouldn't be an easy trip, especially since Mary had a baby inside her.

When they got to Bethlehem, there was no place for them to stay. All the rooms in all of the inns had been taken. So, the only place they could find was a stable. A stable was a tiny house where someone would keep their horses, cows, goats or sheep. It had a roof and maybe one side that was closed but the rest was open to the outside. A stable wouldn't have been a nice place to stay because the animals were smelly, it only had a dirt floor, and it was cold in the winter. There weren't any nice chairs or tables or a bed to sleep on.

And so Jesus, the son of God, was born in a stable. He didn't even have nice clothes to wear. His mom wrapped Him in strips of cloth they'd brought with them because they were too poor to buy Him any clothes. And He also didn't have a nice bed to sleep in. His parents put him to sleep in a manger, which is a box that was used to feed the animals with. Can you imagine what it would be like if you had to sleep in a box that just a few hours earlier had been filled with hay and corn?

Just after Jesus was born in the stable in Bethlehem, an angel visited a number of shepherds who were watching their sheep and goats in the fields. The angel told them about Jesus and how He would save the world from their sins (bad things people do.) The shepherds were amazed at what the angel said.

The angel also said that they would find the baby lying in a manger wrapped in some cloths in Bethlehem. Suddenly, a lot of angels—maybe a million or more!—appeared to gave thanks to God for bringing Jesus into the world. Now the shepherds really believed what they were told about Jesus.

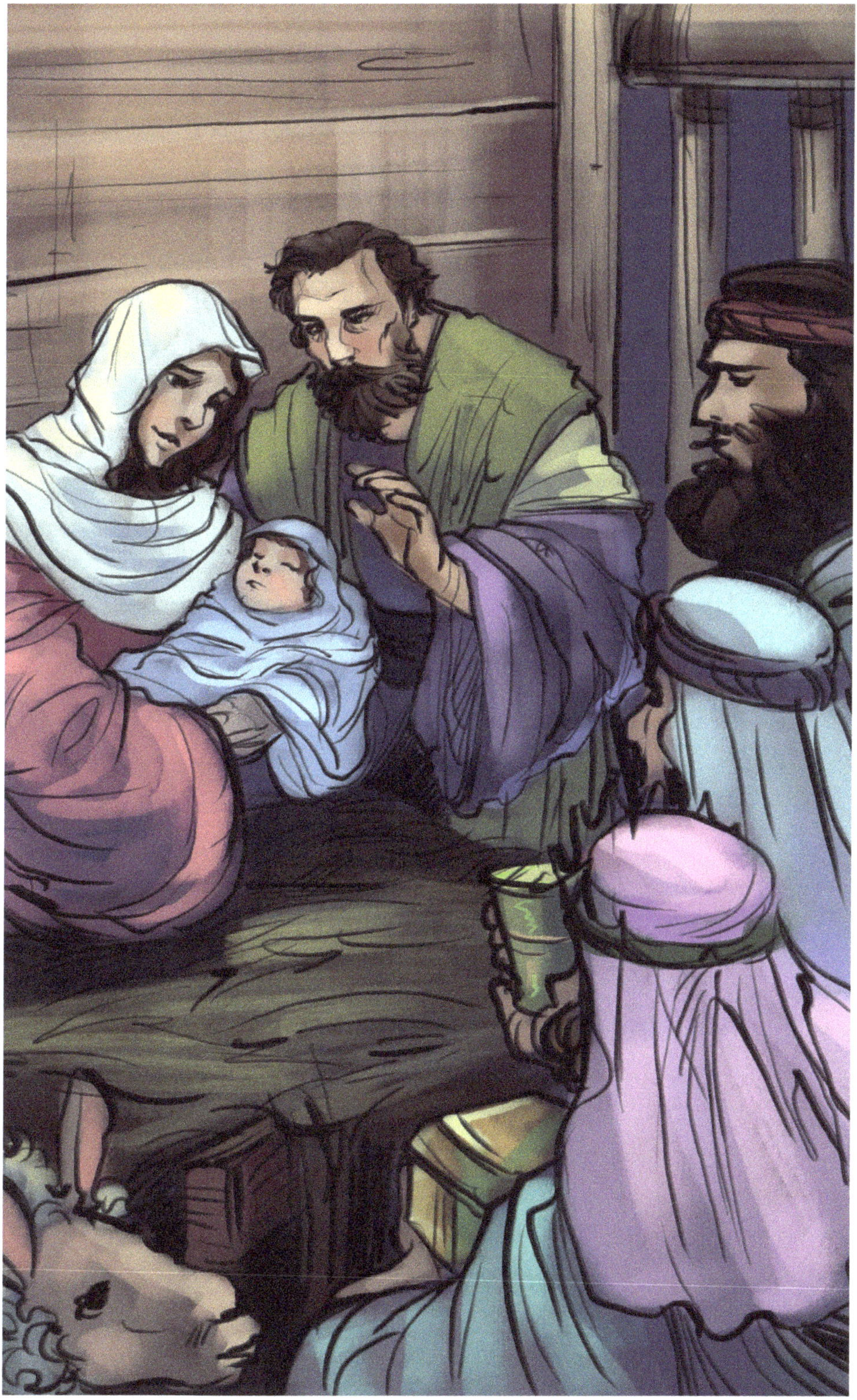

BIBLE ADVENTURE STORIES

Imagine how God felt about his son being born. He couldn't wait to tell everyone so He told the first people He saw—the shepherds. And He had a ton of his angels show up, not just one or two, to tell the great news.

So the shepherds went to the town and found Jesus just the way the angel said they would. He was in a stable, wrapped in cloth and lying in a manger. They were so excited to see Jesus that they ran and told others about him and about what the angel said to them.

Other people showed up, too. Some wise men, called the Magi, came to see Jesus as well. They were men from far away who had been watching the stars for a long time. They saw one that was different from all the rest and believed that it was a sign from God that something special was going to happen.

They loaded up their camels with food and clothing and followed the star until it stopped over Bethlehem. They went to the stable where the shepherds had gone. They saw baby Jesus and they knew He was special. They gave thanks to God and gave Jesus gifts of gold and expensive spices to help take care of Him. Then they returned home with joy in their hearts because they had seen the son of God.

BIBLE ADVENTURE STORIES

That's the story of Jesus' birth. God made the event super special and it was a magical time for Jesus' parents, the people in Bethlehem and the wise men. It was also a special time for God too, because He was able to show us how much He loved us, by sending us His son.

> *"This is how much God loved the world: He gave his Son, his one and only Son. And this is why: so that no one need be destroyed; but by believing in him, anyone can have a whole and lasting life.*
>
> **John 3:16**
> **MSG**

JESUS BATTLES SATAN

MATTHEW 4, LUKE CHAPTER 4

After Jesus had grown up and become a man, Satan, the devil, came to tempt Him. Remember Satan from the story about Job? He was the bad angel who was jealous of God but God threw him out of heaven. And just like he did with Job, Satan spends his time going all over the world tempting people; which means he tries to get people to sin by doing bad things.

We can't see the devil but he's like a voice inside our heads that tries to get us to do wrong things. He wants us to do the wrong things instead of the right things because he wants to hurt God by hurting us.

Well, Jesus had been in the desert, and He fasted for forty days and nights. Fasting is a way that we honor God by not eating anything for a period of time. So by this time, Jesus hadn't eaten anything and He was really hungry. I know I'd be crazy hungry (and tired) if I didn't have anything to eat for forty days!

Then Satan appeared and told Jesus, "If you're really the son of God, turn these stones into bread." Satan wanted Jesus to break his fast and dishonor God. Jesus probably remembered what freshly baked bread smelled like too, and I'll bet He really wanted some.

"No way," said Jesus. "God's word is the only food that I need to fill me up."

That made Satan mad. So he took Jesus to the top of the highest building in Jerusalem. "Why don't you jump off this building, because God says He won't let you be hurt. In fact, He's going to send angels to catch you."

By asking this, Satan wanted Jesus to doubt that God loved Him and to doubt in God's promise to protect and save Him.

Jesus looked at the ground, which was really far away. Jesus knew that God would rescue Him if He jumped. But instead of testing God, Jesus answered, "God also says not to test Him, but to trust in all of His promises."

That made the devil even madder than before. Finally, the devil took Jesus to the top of a high mountain and showed him all the kingdoms of the world. Satan said, "I'll give all of these to you if you'll bow down and give me praise and honor."

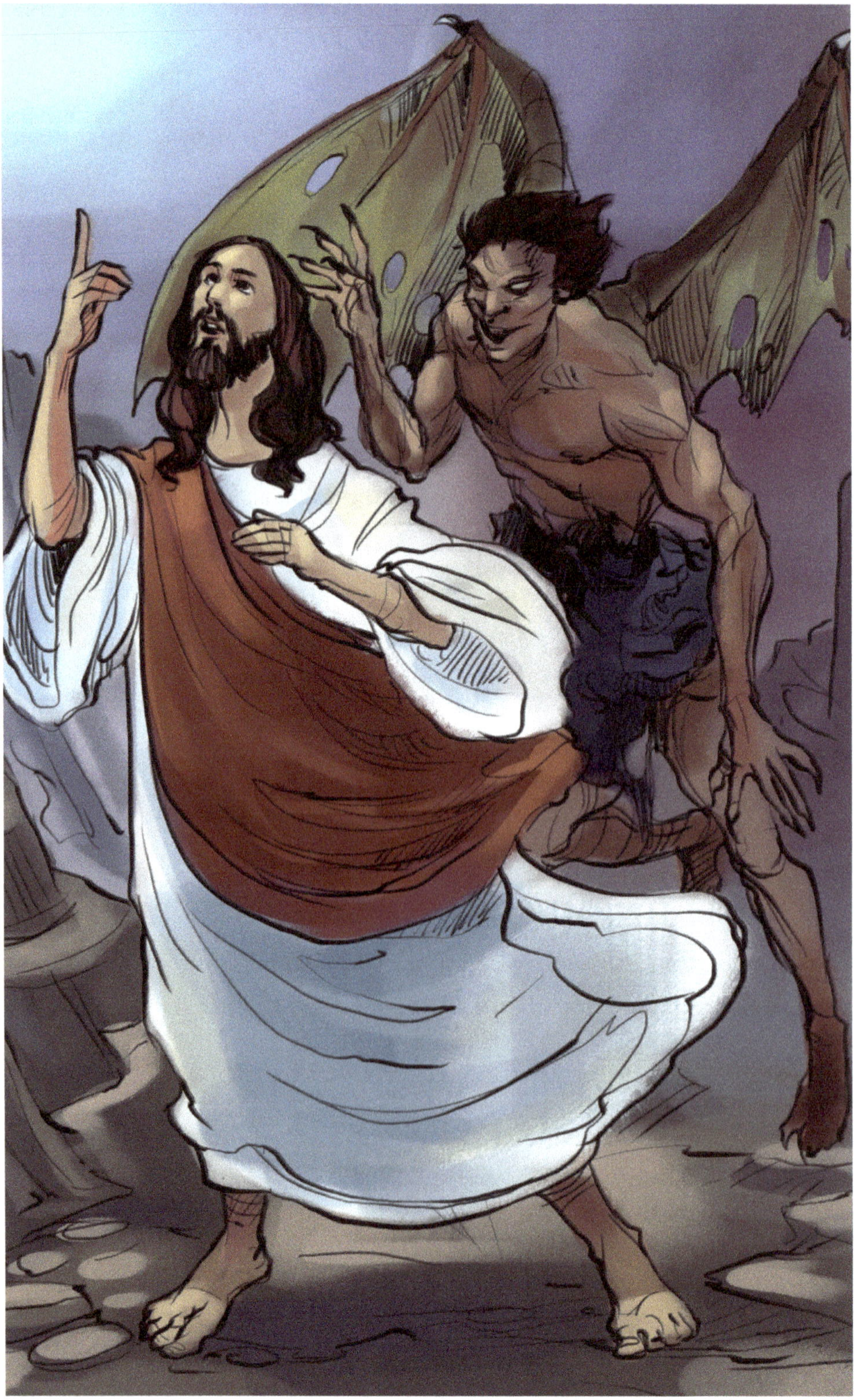

Now, one thing you must know is that Satan is a liar and can only tell lies. He never tells the truth. So it was a lie that he said he could give all the kingdoms of the world to Jesus when he really couldn't.

Jesus had enough of the devil and told him, "Get away from me, Satan! The Bible says to only give praise and honor to God and to believe in Him alone." And because Jesus said it with so much power, He scared Satan away.

Wow! Look at how strong Jesus was. Satan tempted Him but Jesus fought back with the words of God and the devil had to run away. When Satan tries to get us to do something wrong, we can do that too. We can pray and ask Jesus to make Satan leave and he will because God is stronger than the devil.

> *Submit yourselves, then, to God. Resist the devil, and he will flee from you.*
>
> **James 4:7**
> **NIV**

> *But the Lord is faithful, and He will strengthen and protect you from the evil one.*
>
> **2 Thessalonians 3:3**
> **NIV**

JESUS HEALS THE LEPER

MARK CHAPTER 1

One day, a man with leprosy came to Jesus, got down on his knees and begged for Jesus to heal him. "If you are willing," he said, "you can make me clean."

Before we go on with this story, you should know what leprosy is. It's a disease that attacks a person's skin. Ugly, nasty sores can appear from your head to your feet. Then these sores get infected and grow. People can lose their fingers and toes, even their noses or their ears. They were usually covered in bandages.

It's sad, but people with leprosy (called lepers) were scary to look at and everyone stayed away from them. What's more, the disease is contagious, so if you touched a leper you could get leprosy yourself! Because of this lepers always had to live far away from other people. If anyone came close to them, lepers would have to shout from a distance, "Unclean! Unclean!" so that everyone would know they shouldn't come near them.

BIBLE ADVENTURE STORIES

We have medicine that can cure leprosy today. But there was no cure for leprosy in Jesus' time. This meant that there was no hope for lepers. They would never get well and would only get worse over time. Since they couldn't live near anyone else, lepers often lived together and would help each other as best they could.

Picture what it must have been like if you had leprosy back then. You would be very sad, lonely and afraid. You couldn't play with your friends or see your parents any more. You would feel ashamed every time you saw a normal person because you'd have to tell them to stay away. You looked and felt terrible.

When this leper heard that Jesus was coming, he must have heard stories about Jesus healing sick people. He wanted to get excited but he wasn't' sure. Would Jesus heal him? Could Jesus heal him? He would have to break the rules that said he wasn't allowed to go near other people if he wanted to see Jesus. The man decided he was going to try no matter what. Jesus was his only hope.

So he went up to Jesus and asked him to make him well again. Jesus looked at him, saw that he was a leper and Jesus knew what his life must have been like. This man hadn't been touched for many years. But, Jesus cared deeply for this man and had power from God to make

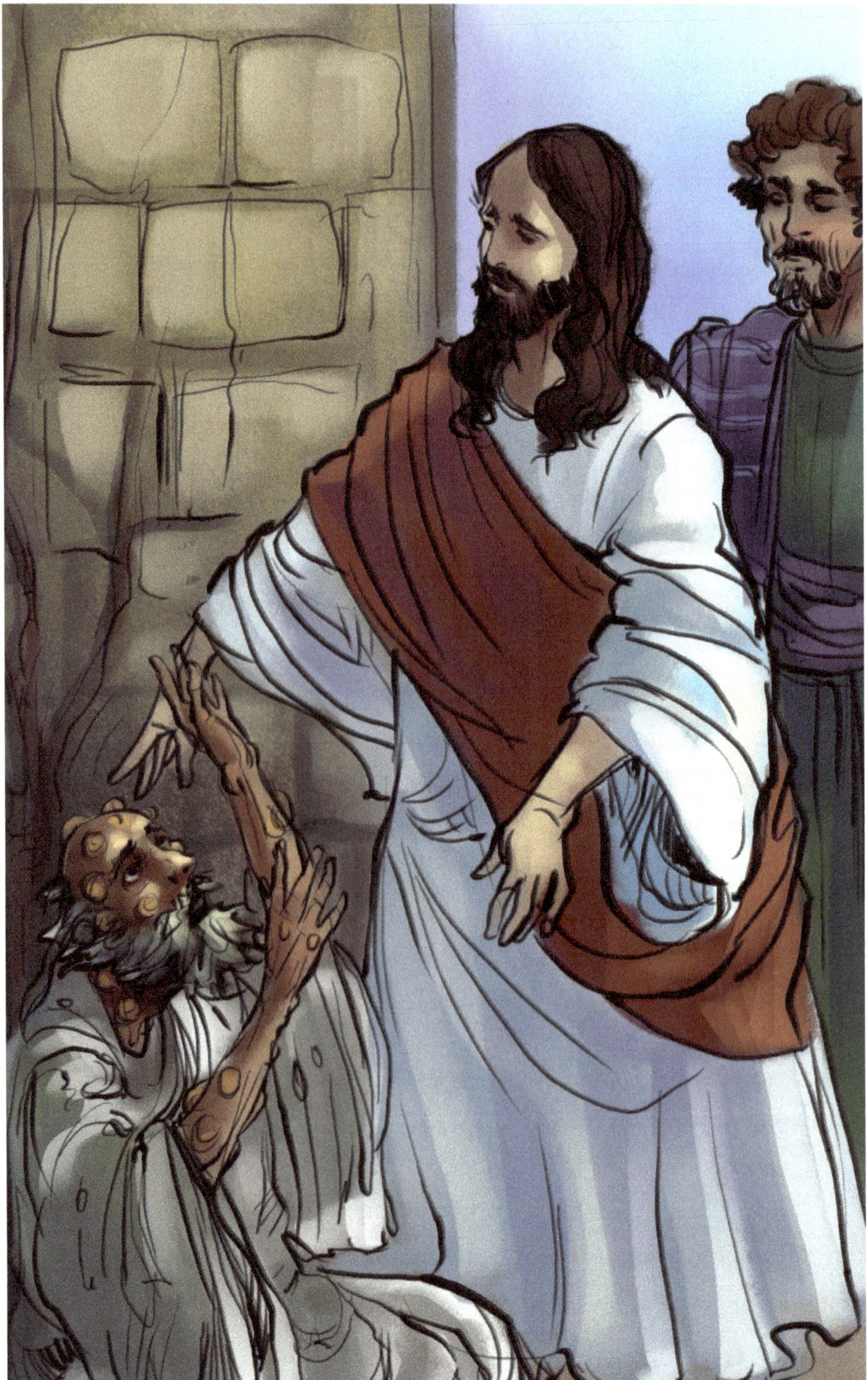

him well. So Jesus reached out his hand, and touched the man saying, "I am willing. Be clean!"

Now Jesus could've healed the leper from far away, but Jesus wanted the man to feel the touch of a human being again. People around Jesus must've thought that Jesus was crazy. But, Jesus had so much compassion for this man, that He didn't care what people thought and reached out and touched him.

At once, the leper was cured. His disease was gone! His skin was smooth and clean again. He could stand up straight and he felt good on the inside. He hooped and hollered because he was well. He was able to see his family and friends again. He was so happy and excited about the miracle Jesus had done for him that he went all over the countryside telling people about it.

If we're sick or lonely or sad, we can go to Jesus in prayer and ask Him to make us better. It's wonderful to know that Jesus cares about all of us and wants us to be well.

> *The LORD is gracious and righteous; our God is full of compassion.*
>
> **Psalms 116:5**
> **NIV**

JESUS CALMS THE STORM

MATTHEW CHAPTER 8, MARK CHAPTER 4, LUKE CHAPTER 8

Jesus spent most of his days teaching people about God. On a certain day, He was by a lake. The crowd was so large that He got in a boat, rowed it out from the shore and talked to the people from there. The crowd sat on the beach.

Jesus taught all day long and when it was almost night, He said to his friends, "Let's go to the other side of the lake." They all piled into the boat and before long, Jesus was so tired that He fell asleep on a cushion in the back of the boat.

Meanwhile, a big storm arose. Now, this was no ordinary storm. This one was really strong, with high winds and big waves. The boat was tossed back and forth on the lake. A number of times it almost turned over.

The men saw they were in danger and were afraid. They hoped Jesus could help them.

They looked to see what Jesus was doing. But Jesus was fast asleep in the middle of the storm! How could He be sleeping when they were in major trouble? So they went to wake Him up. "Jesus," they cried, "Wake up! Can't you see that we're in trouble? Don't you care if we drown?" They were really afraid that they weren't going to make it.

Jesus stood up, looked around at everything that was going on, and then said to the wind, "Be quiet!" and to the waves, "Be still!" Suddenly, everything was calm. The wind died down and the water became still.

Jesus turned to his friends and said, "What were you afraid of? Don't you believe that I am God's son, and that God cares for you and wouldn't let you drown?"

The men stared at each other. "Whoa! Who is this guy? He can even tell the wind and the waves to be still and they obey Him."

Now, I would have been scared too. Wouldn't you? Jesus looked just like a normal man, but He was special. His friends knew there was something special about him, but they weren't sure. After Jesus calmed the storm, He

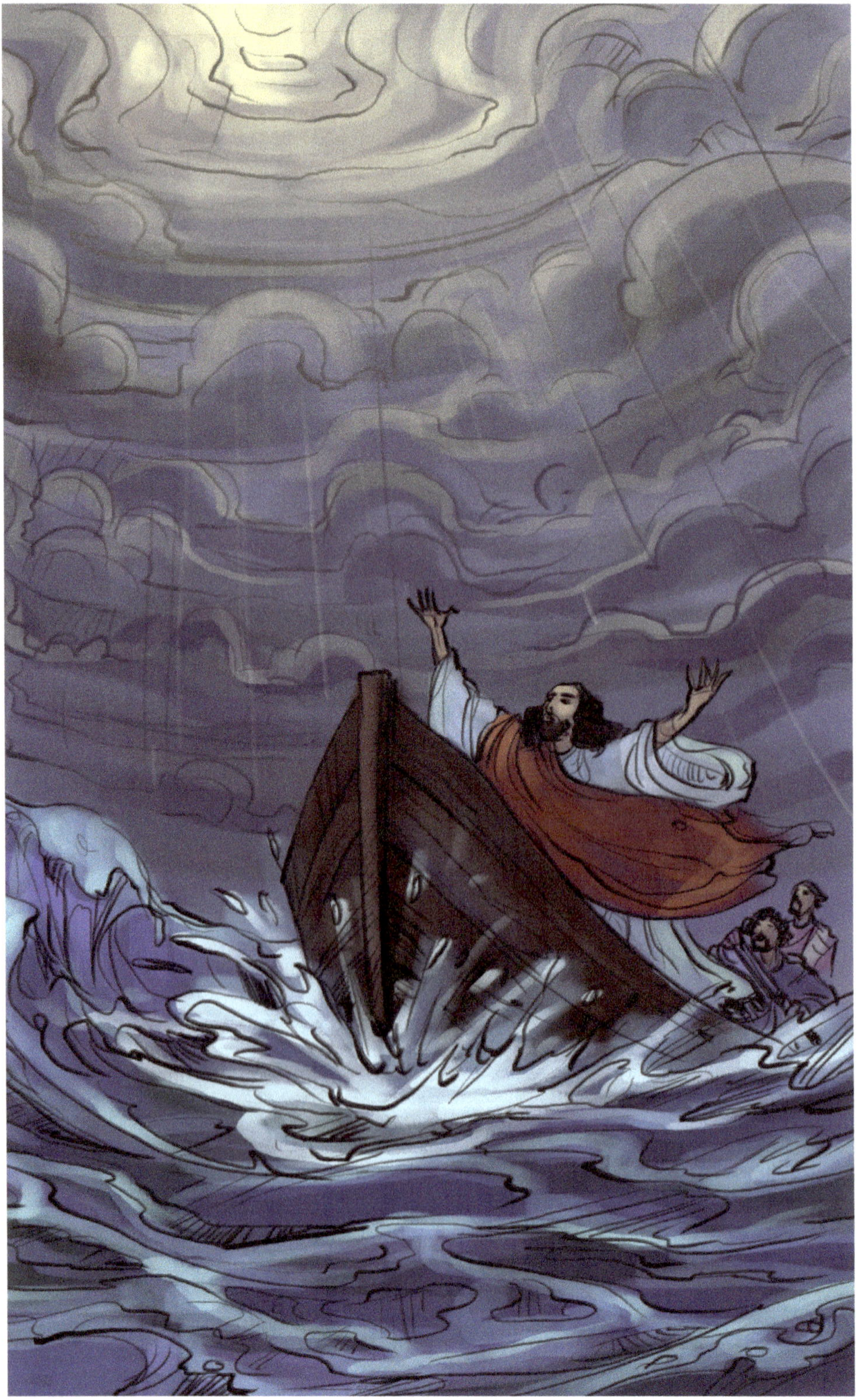

BIBLE ADVENTURE STORIES

simply blew their minds! They were surer than ever that He was the son of God after He did that.

We have storms in our lives, too. They may not be real storms like the one Jesus and his friends faced. But they're real to us. And we can worry about those storms like Jesus' friends did.

But, just like Jesus helped His friends, He can come to our rescue as well. All we need to do is come to Him for help.

> *So do not worry, saying, 'What shall we eat?' or 'What shall we drink?' or 'What shall we wear?' For the pagans run after all these things, and your heavenly Father knows that you need them. But seek first His kingdom and His righteousness, and all these things will be given to you as well.*
>
> **Matthew 6:31-34**
> **NIV**

JESUS FEEDS THE FIVE THOUSAND

MATTHEW CHAPTER 14, MARK CHAPTER 6, LUKE CHAPTER 9, JOHN CHAPTER 6

Jesus had become well known in the area where He lived and many people came to see Him. He would make sick people better and would tell everyone about God. He taught his closest friends to also share with others about God and the good things Jesus told them.

One day, they were so busy they didn't even have time to eat! Jesus noticed that and said, "Hey guys. We need a break. Let's go someplace where we can rest for a while." They got in a boat and rowed to the other side, thinking it would be quiet when they got there.

Instead, when they landed, a huge crowd was waiting. The people brought their sick friends and family because they heard that Jesus could make people well. When Jesus saw the sick people, He felt sorry for them, touched them and made them all better. Then He went up on a hillside and told everyone the good news about God's kingdom and what it was like.

By the time He finished talking, it was late in the afternoon. No one had eaten anything and they were all hungry. "Where should we get food for all these people?" Jesus asked. One of his friends, Philip, said, "Even if someone worked for eight months, they wouldn't make enough money to give each person one bite." Jesus' other friends said that He should send the people away to nearby towns to get food.

But Jesus was worried that some people were too hungry and too tired to do that. "Why don't you feed them?" Jesus replied. His friends looked at each other. They were all thinking the same thing. "What's He talking about?" they thought. "We don't have any food. Is Jesus messing with us or what?"

Andrew spoke up. "There's a kid here who has five small loaves of bread and two small fish, but that won't feed all these people." Then they were all quiet and wondered what to do next.

"Have everyone sit down in small groups," Jesus ordered. While they were doing that, Jesus looked up to heaven and thanked God for the bread and fish. Then

He broke them into pieces and gave them to his friends to pass out. They used baskets to carry the food and they gave it to the people who were there. As they were giving out the food, everyone became aware that a miracle was happening because the bread and fish never ran out!

After all the people were full, Jesus wanted his friends to bring back the leftovers. When they had finished collecting the leftovers, they filled twelve baskets full, even though they only started with five small loaves of bread and two fish. Jesus fed five thousand men that day, plus women and children!

Only after everyone had eaten did Jesus send them away. And they were all amazed at the miracle that took place.

Can you imagine what they told their friends when they got home? "Wow! You're not going to believe this but there were thousands of us in the middle of nowhere listening to this guy Jesus talk about God. He spoke until it was dinner time and we were all hungry. The only food there was a few loaves of bread and a couple of fish. Jesus thanked God for the food and they passed it around and it never ran out! Everybody ate until they were stuffed. I've never seen anything like that before."

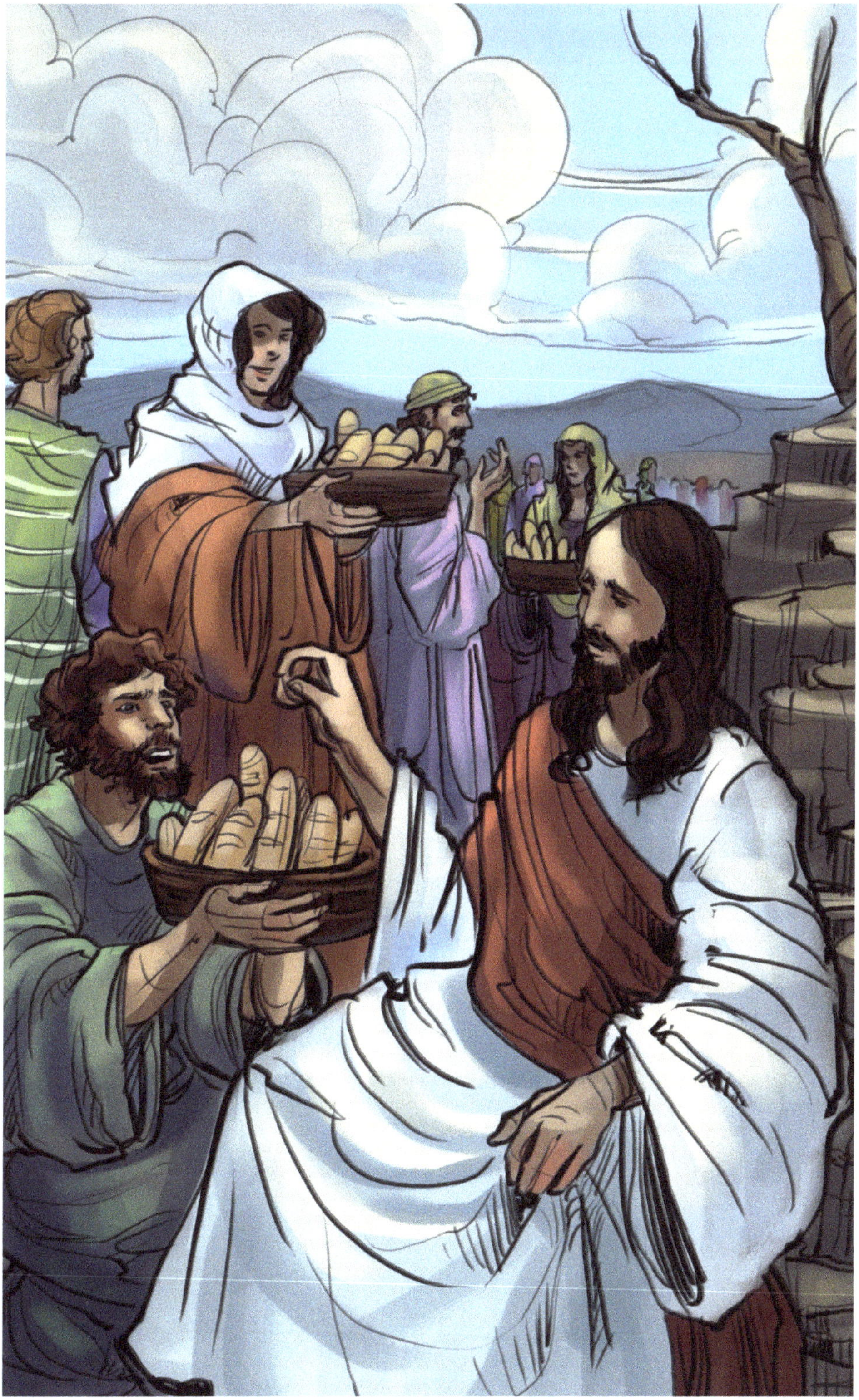

BIBLE ADVENTURE STORIES

Just like with Jesus, God will provide for us, if we just follow Him and ask Him for help.

> *You can be sure that God will take care of everything you need...*
>
> **Philippians 4:19**
> **MSG**

JESUS WALKS ON WATER

MATTHEW CHAPTER 14, JOHN CHAPTER 6, MARK CHAPTER 6

After Jesus did the miracle of feeding thousands of people, He had his friends get in a boat and told them He'd meet them on the other side of the lake. They started rowing across the lake while Jesus went up on a mountain to pray. He often prayed by himself for a long time. It was how Jesus stayed close to God.

About three o'clock in the morning, after He finished praying, Jesus decided to cross the lake himself. But He didn't use a boat like his friends did, or like you and I would. He just walked on the water—and He didn't sink!

Now, you're probably thinking, "No way! Nobody can do that." Well, Jesus did. Remember, Jesus was the son of God, so he wasn't an ordinary person like us. He could do things no one else could do because God gave him special power.

So Jesus started walking out onto the lake. He could see the boat his friends were in. They hadn't gotten very far because the wind was blowing against them. It was almost morning and they still hadn't reached the other side.

When Jesus got near the boat, His friends saw Him and they got really scared. "It's a ghost!" they shouted. Jesus heard them and replied, "Hey, it's not a ghost. It's me. Don't be afraid."

Now, I don't know about you, but if I saw a guy walking on water I would be pretty scared too.

Peter, one of the guys in the boat, called out to him. "If it's really you, Jesus, tell me to come out to you." I don't know what Peter was thinking, but he was probably scared out of his wits and didn't know what to say. So he probably just said the first thing that popped into his head.

"Ok, Peter, come here," Jesus called. I'm sure Peter wasn't expecting Jesus to say that! But, Peter did it. He put one leg over the side of the boat and touched the water with his foot. It got wet but he didn't sink. Then he put his other leg over the side of the boat and put it on the water, too. He still didn't sink.

BIBLE ADVENTURE STORIES

"This is cool," he must have thought. So he started out toward Jesus, walking on the water just as Jesus did. But then he felt the wind blowing and saw that the waves were really big. He must've thought, "This is impossible, a man can't do this. I'm going to drown out here in the water."

Then Peter got scared and he started to sink. He cried out to Jesus, "Save me, Lord!"

Jesus reached out His hand and caught him. "Peter, what happened to your faith?" Jesus asked. "Why did you doubt that you could do it?"

Just then they reached the boat and they both climbed in. The other guys who were in the boat with Peter were amazed at Jesus. "You must be the Son of God," they said. They knew that only God himself was able to give Jesus the power to walk on water.

I think hanging out with Jesus would have been fun because you never knew what He was going to do next. But whatever He did, it really helped his friends trust that God loved them and that God was powerful.

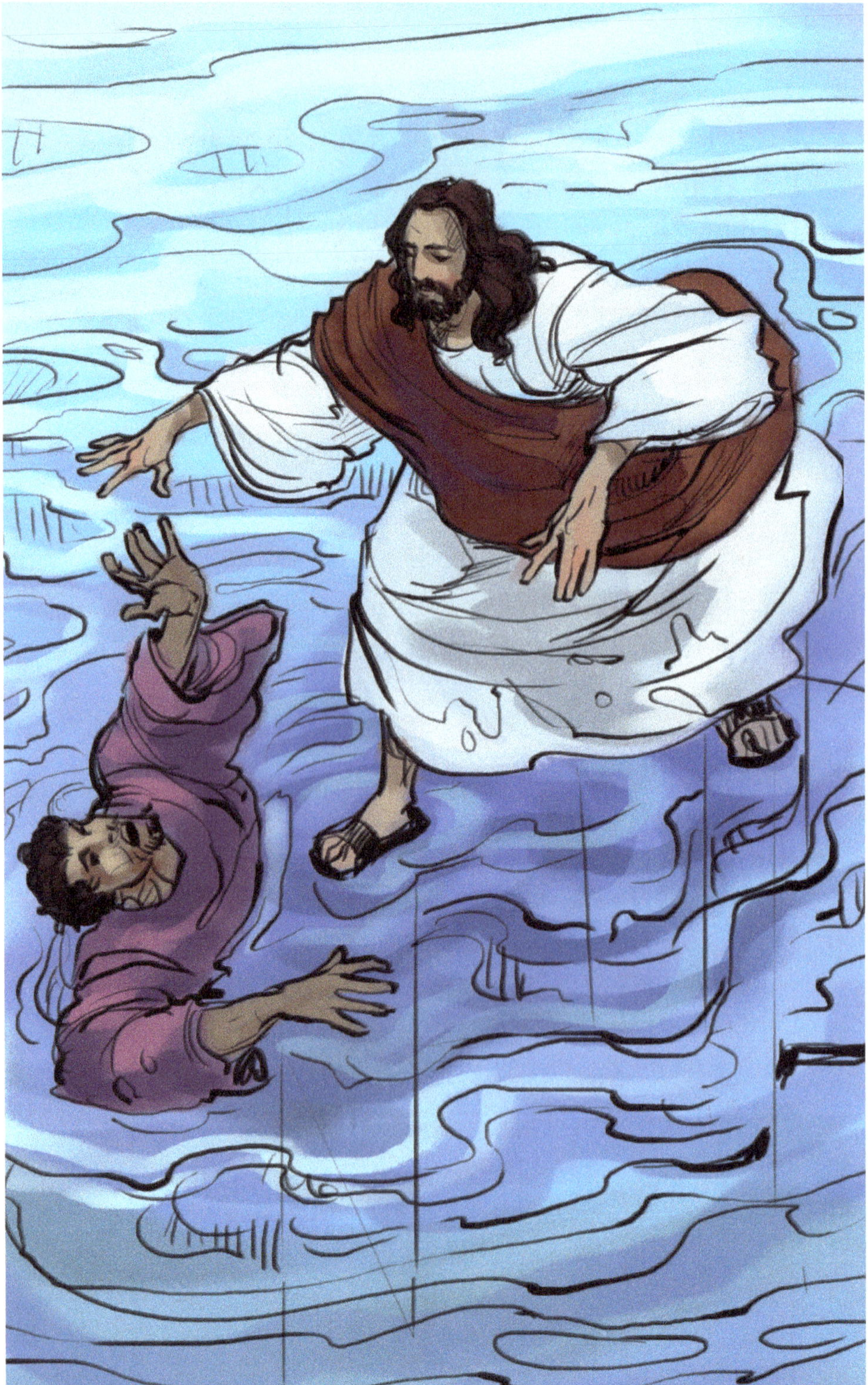

BIBLE ADVENTURE STORIES

God cares about us just as much as He did Jesus' friends. Also God is just as powerful now as He was then. What amazing things do you think God can do in your life, if you just ask Him?

> *Looking at them, Jesus said, "With people it is impossible, but not with God; for all things are possible with God."*
>
> **Mark 10:27**
> **NIV**

JESUS FACES A MAN CALLED LEGION

MATTHEW CHAPTER 8, MARK CHAPTER 5, LUKE CHAPTER 8

Once again Jesus took a boat to another town that was near Lake Galilee. When He got out, a man ran up to Jesus. Now this was no ordinary man. This man lived in a graveyard and he was very dangerous. He was very sad and angry, and spent his time scaring all the people who lived near him. From time to time, some of the people would even tie him up with chains on both his hands and feet because he was so dangerous. But he was so strong that he would break his chains and run away into the countryside.

He was that way because his brain didn't work right. He listened to what evil spirits told him instead of what good spirits told him. Do you remember the story of

Job? There was that day when the angels showed up before God and a bad angel, Satan, also came.

Well, angels and spirits are kind of the same thing. There are good angels, like Gabriel, and then there are bad angels, like Satan.

Angels, or spirits, try to get you to do good things or bad things. They put ideas in your mind to do what's right or to do what's wrong. In the case of this man, there were a lot of evil spirits who were putting bad ideas into his head.

When Jesus landed on the lake shore, the evil spirits knew who He was, that He was the Son of God. Just as in Job's story, God rules over all spirits, including evil ones. That's why the man with the evil spirits ran up to Jesus. And when Jesus saw him, He commanded the evil spirits to leave the man alone. The evil spirits inside the man made the man shout at the top of his voice, "What do you want with us, Jesus, Son of the Most High God?"

"What's your name?" Jesus asked the evil spirits.

"Legion," the evil spirits replied, "because we are many." This poor man was held prisoner in his head by many evil spirits, perhaps hundreds, or even thousands.

The evil spirits begged Jesus not to send them out of the area. Nearby was a huge herd of pigs, about 2,000 in number. The evil spirits asked Jesus if He would let them go into the pigs. "Go," Jesus answered, and the spirits left the man and entered the pigs.

When evil spirits went into the pigs, all the pigs went crazy, rushed down the hill, jumped in the lake and drowned.

This really scared the villagers who were tending the pigs. So, they ran into the town and told everyone about what they saw. All the people were afraid and they went out to where Jesus and the man were to see for themselves what happened. They found the man they normally thought was crazy, and they saw him sitting quietly with Jesus. He was dressed and in his right mind again! Jesus had totally healed him.

You would think the people would be happy that the man was well and that he would never scare them again. Instead, they were afraid of what else might happen with Jesus there. They cared more about their drowned pigs than the man Jesus made better. So they asked Jesus to go away.

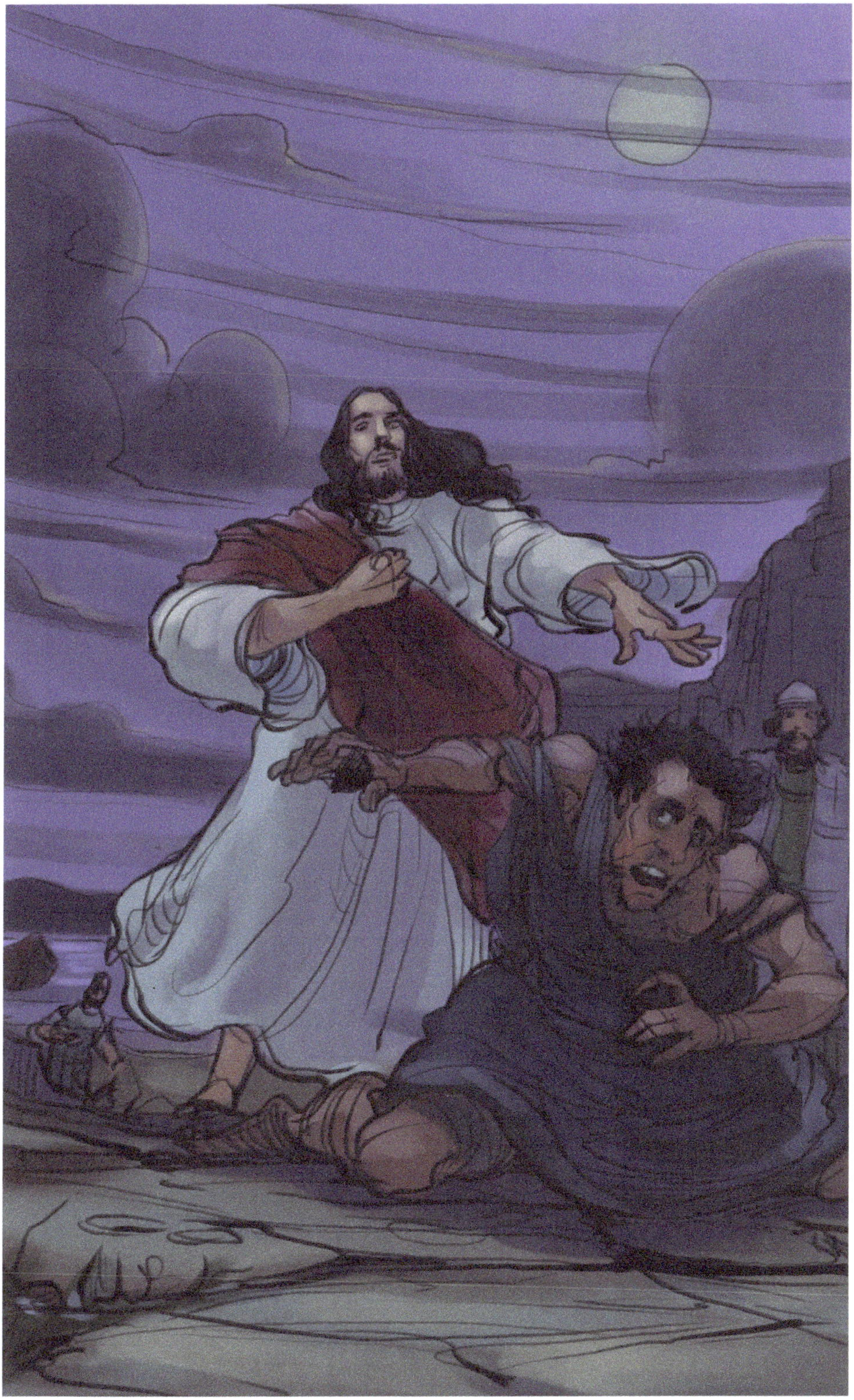

BIBLE ADVENTURE STORIES

As Jesus was getting in the boat, the man begged to go with him. He was grateful for what Jesus had done for him. Instead, Jesus said he should go back to his family and tell them how good God was to him. The man was so happy that he didn't just go to his own town but he went to ten towns to tell everyone there about what Jesus did for him.

> "...Be strong and courageous. Do not be terrified; do not be discouraged, for the LORD your God will be with you wherever you go."
>
> **Joshua 1:9**
> **NIV**

JESUS RAISES LAZARUS FROM THE DEAD

JOHN CHAPTER 11

Jesus had three good friends named Mary, Martha and Lazarus. Mary and Martha were sisters and Lazarus was their brother. They lived in a small town called Bethany.

Lazarus became sick and the sisters sent a message to Jesus asking him to come visit them. They knew that Jesus could make Lazarus well. At that time, Jesus was in the city of Jerusalem, which was only a few miles from Bethany. There were other things He needed to do in that place so He stayed in Jerusalem for a few more days.

Jesus loved Mary, Martha and Lazarus. So when He finished what He was doing, He went out to Bethany to see them. When He reached the town, He learned that Lazarus died and had already been buried for four days. Martha heard that Jesus was coming so she went out to meet Him. When she found him she said, "Lord, if You had been here, You could have healed my brother. And even now I know that God will give you whatever you ask of Him."

Jesus told her, "Your brother will rise again."

Martha didn't understand what Jesus meant but she said, "I believe You are the Son of God, the one that the Bible said would come to teach us the truth."

Then Martha returned home and told her sister that Jesus had come. They had many friends who had come from Jerusalem to be with them during this sad time. Once Mary found out that Jesus was there, she went to see him. Martha and their friends went with her. When Mary reached him, she said the same thing to Jesus that Martha had said: "Lord, if You had been here, You could have healed my brother."

Mary, Martha and their friends were crying. They were sad that Lazarus had died and that they would never see him again. Jesus felt their pain and sadness. He asked to see where Lazarus had been buried. Then Jesus cried, too.

You may know how those people felt. Perhaps someone in your family died, like your grandma or an uncle, or even your mom or brother. If not, maybe your family dog or cat died. You think about how much you loved them and all the good times you had with them. But now they're gone and that makes you very sad because they can't be with you anymore. That's how Mary, Martha and their friends felt about Lazarus.

When they all got to the tomb (the place where Lazarus had been buried), Jesus looked up to heaven and said, "Father, I thank You because you always hear Me. Please show Your power now so that the people who are here with Me will believe in You." Then Jesus called out in a loud voice, "Lazarus, come out!"

And then the most amazing thing happened. Lazarus came out of the tomb. He was alive!

Can you imagine how everyone must have felt? The sisters must have been filled with joy that their brother was well again. Their friends would have felt the same way. And all the people would have been shocked by what took place. No one had ever heard of someone being raised from the dead before.

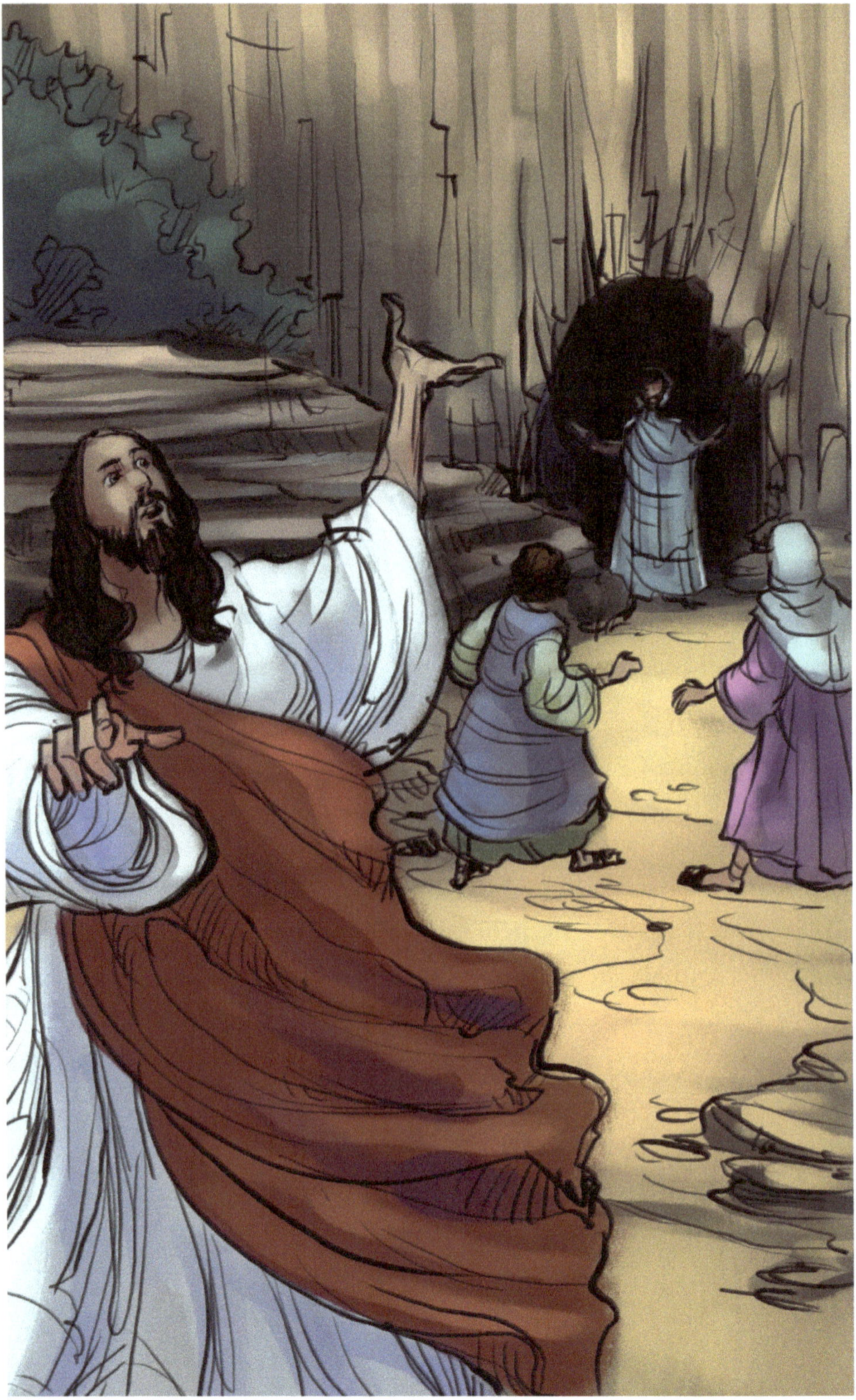

BIBLE ADVENTURE STORIES

But that's what Jesus can do because He cares about our feelings and He cares what happens to us. He has the power to make sick people well. And if we believe in Him and obey His words, He'll even make us alive with God forever in heaven one day.

> *This is what my Father wants: that anyone who sees the Son and trusts who he is and what he does and then [follows] him will [get] eternal life.*
>
> **John 6:40**
> **MSG**

JESUS CLEANSES THE TEMPLE

MATTHEW CHAPTER 21, MARK CHAPTER 11, LUKE CHAPTER 19, JOHN CHAPTER 2

During the time of Jesus, the Jews had a special building called the temple. It was the place where they worshipped God. That meant that they prayed there, teachers taught them about God there, and they sang songs to God. It was like their church.

There was only one temple and it was in Jerusalem, the most important city in Israel. It was the one place on earth where God said He would live. We know that God really lives in heaven but He wanted to have a home on earth where He could be close to his people.

Since God is so amazing, His house was, too. It was a huge building and there was nothing else like it in the entire world. It was very tall and wide and the roof was held up by big columns. The fancy decorations were covered in shiny gold and only people with special skills could work on the temple.

The Jews would bring gifts to God that helped the people who took care of the temple. Instead of money, most people brought animals like cows and sheep. If they were really poor, they brought birds, like doves. If someone had money, they would bring that also.

The temple had been around for a long time when Jesus saw it, and it was amazing. The men who had worked on it did a great job, and it made Jesus happy to see all the care that had gone into it.

But He saw something that day that made him very sad. He saw lots of people selling animals and cheating people out of their money. It was also noisy, dirty and smelly. This was not what God wanted when He had the temple built. It was supposed to be a special place where people could worship God. Instead, it was more like a market with people shouting, people being cheated out of their money and animals making all kinds of noises.

Can you picture what it would be like if this happened in your house? Imagine you go on vacation with your parents and when you come back, there's a cow in your living room! There are sheep in your bedroom. And people you've never seen before are walking through your house shouting the prices of the animals they're selling.

You'd wonder what was going on. The house was fine when you left and now it was simply crazy! Your parents would probably be really mad at everyone and start yelling at them to leave and take their animals and birds with them. Sometimes it's OK to be mad when people are doing the wrong thing.

Well, Jesus was mad at what He saw in the temple, too. He made a whip out of pieces of rope and He drove the animals out. He turned over the tables of the people who were selling stuff and cheating people. He let the doves out of their cages. He threw them all out of the temple because it was God's house and it was supposed to be treated with special honor.

That's how it should be today when we go to church. Church should be a place where we go to think about God and how good He is to us. We go there to pray, learn about God and sing songs to Him. We should treat it like a very special place because it's God's house and we always want to make God feel special.

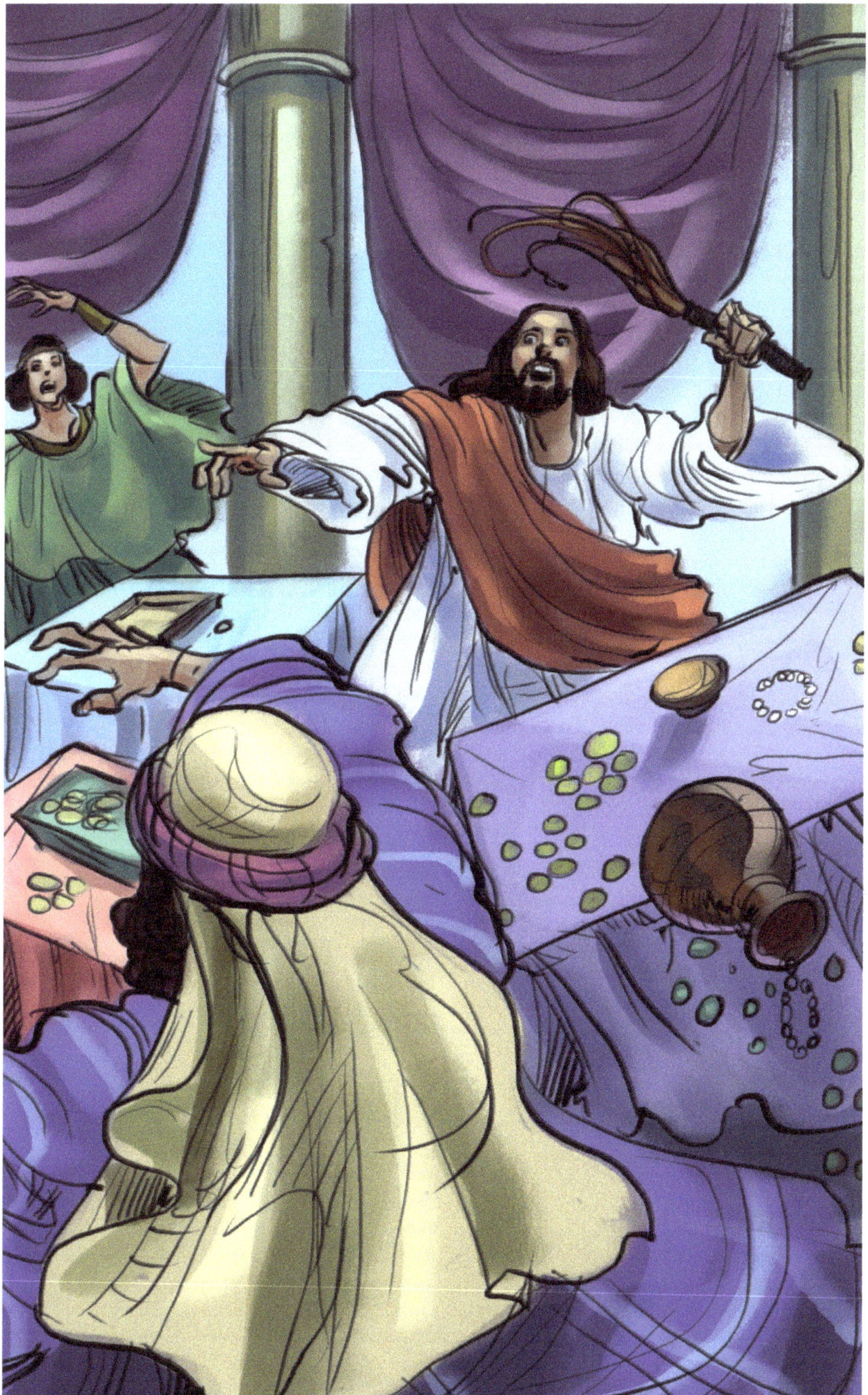

BIBLE ADVENTURE STORIES

I write so that you will know how one ought to conduct himself in the household of God, which is the church of the living God...

1 Timothy 3:15
NASB

JESUS DIES AND RISES FROM THE DEAD

MATTHEW CHAPTERS 26-28, MARK CHAPTERS 14-16, LUKE CHAPTERS 22-24, JOHN CHAPTERS 18-20

Jesus knew that the time had come for Him to leave the earth and to go to heaven. So, He met with His closest friends to have dinner. This was the last time Jesus would eat dinner with His friends while He was alive, so it was a very special time for all of them.

Unfortunately, one the men there named Judas had agreed to help Jesus' enemies capture him. So he left during the meal to help Jesus's enemies get ready.

You're probably wondering why Jesus had enemies, when all He did was spend time doing good and helping people. Well, Satan convinced many people that Jesus was bad. So these people wanted to arrest Jesus and get rid of Him permanently. So these enemies of Jesus convinced Judas, one of Jesus's friends, to betray Him by paying Judas thirty pieces of silver.

Now, after dinner, Jesus went with His friends to a place where He could pray and He asked them to pray for Him as well. He was afraid of what was going to happen to Him once his enemies found Him. So He asked God to give Him strength.

When He was done, a large crowd of men with clubs and spears came to take Jesus prisoner. Judas was with them and he pointed out which one was Jesus. They grabbed Jesus. His friends were very afraid, and ran away. Jesus had to face His enemies alone.

They took Him to the house of the leader of Jesus' enemies. There was a crowd there of people that didn't like Jesus, and were jealous of Him. These were the men who gave Jesus a hard time when He taught the people about God. They didn't believe Jesus was the Son of God and wanted to keep Him from teaching any more.

The next day, Jesus' enemies took Jesus to the man in charge of Jerusalem, named Pilate. Pilate was like the mayor of the city of Jerusalem. Jesus' enemies accused Jesus of doing all kinds of wrongs things (which wasn't true). They even made up stories about how Jesus was a king who was trying to overthrow the Roman government. The Romans were the nation ruling Jerusalem at the time.

Pilate asked if it was true that Jesus was a king. "Yes," Jesus replied. But Jesus was talking about being a king in heaven, not here on earth.

After questioning him, Pilate knew that Jesus was not guilty of the crimes Jesus' enemies had accused him of. So Pilate tried to set Jesus free. But the Jews kept pushing Pilate to punish Jesus and finally Pilate gave in. He had Jesus beaten with a whip and soldiers punched and hit him. They treated Jesus like He was a criminal.

Then they decided to give Jesus the punishment that was usually reserved for the worst of criminals. They took Jesus to the top of a hill outside the city and nailed His hands and feet to a big wooden cross, which they set upright in the ground.

While Jesus was hanging there, Jesus' enemies came by and made fun of Him. So did the soldiers who were ordered to nail him on the cross. However, many people who believed in Jesus came to see Him and pray for him. Some of his closest friends and family came as well, including his mom. Jesus asked a friend of His to take care of her because He wanted to make sure she would be alright when He was gone.

All of a sudden, from twelve o'clock until three o'clock in the afternoon, darkness came over the entire country, and the sun stopped shining. No one knew what was happening. That's like if you were playing outside during the day and suddenly it got so dark that it looked like its nighttime. This is what happened in Jerusalem, and the people were really scared.

Finally, Jesus died. When He died there was a great earthquake that shook the entire town. One of the soldiers felt the earthquake and thought that maybe Jesus was the Son of God after all.

After Jesus died, two good men who had believed in Jesus went to Pilate and asked if they could take Jesus and bury him. Pilate said 'yes' so they took him down from the cross, washed his wounds and wrapped him in strips of cloth. Then they laid him in a new tomb and rolled a large stone across the front of the tomb so that no one would do anything to Jesus' body.

When the people that followed Jesus went home that night, they were all really sad. It must have seemed like everything went wrong. All Jesus did was tell people the truth about God, teach them the right way to live and heal those who were sick. And some folks had Him killed because they were jealous. It made no sense.

But that's not the end of the story…

Three days later, some women went to Jesus' tomb very early in the morning. When they got there, they saw the stone rolled away. Two angels appeared in white clothes that were as bright as lightning. "Who are you looking for?" one of them asked.

"Jesus," the women replied.

"He's not here. But He's alive!" the angels said. "God raised Him from the dead just like Jesus said He would. Take a look in the tomb for yourselves."

The women poked their heads in and saw Jesus' grave clothes folded up. But Jesus wasn't there.

"Where is He?" they asked.

One of the angels said, "He's in Galilee waiting to see you. Now go and tell His friends to meet him there."

So, the women hurried off. They were filled with joy at the good news that Jesus had risen from the dead.

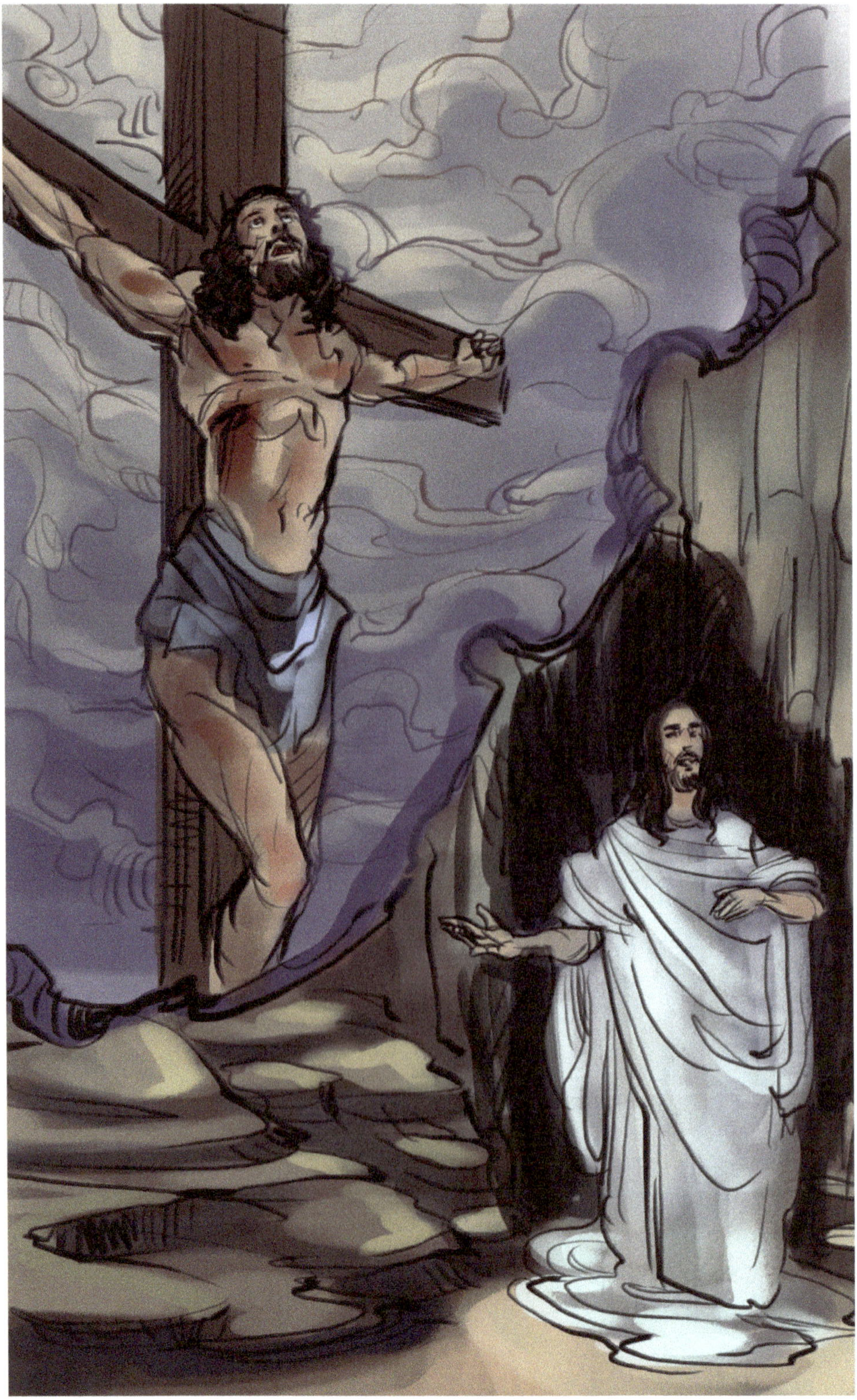

BIBLE ADVENTURE STORIES

When they reached the others, they told them what they had seen and how the two angels told them to go to Galilee to see Jesus. Two of Jesus' friends, Peter and John, ran to the tomb to see for themselves if what the women had told them was right. Everything was just as they said, but they still didn't see Jesus.

Later that day, when all of Jesus' friends were in the same room, Jesus appeared before them. They thought He was a ghost and were frightened.

Jesus said to them, "Don't worry. It's me, Jesus. Come touch Me. See that I'm alive. A ghost doesn't have flesh and bones like I do, does it? By the way, I'm hungry. Do you have anything to eat?"

His friends were so amazed and glad that at first they didn't know what to do. Then they got him some fish and He ate it in front of them.

For about forty days Jesus spent time with His friends so that they would believe that He had truly risen from the dead. He also spent that time teaching his friends about the kingdom of God.

Then one day He told all of his friends to come meet him on a mountain. While there, Jesus gave them one last command before He went back to heaven.

BIBLE ADVENTURE STORIES

Jesus said, "All authority in heaven and on earth has been given to Me. Therefore go and make disciples of all nations, baptizing them in the name of the Father and of the Son and of the Holy Spirit, and teaching them to obey everything I have commanded you. And I will be with you always, to the very end of the age."

And after Jesus said this, He floated up to heaven on a cloud. And Jesus is living in heaven with God to this day.

Jesus wants us to be with Him so that we can be best friends with Him forever, even after we die. All we have to do is believe in Jesus and do what he says in the bible. He also wants us to tell others to love God, so they too, can enjoy being with Jesus and God in heaven forever.

> *"...and He Himself bore our sins in His body on the cross, so that we might die to sin and live to righteousness; for by His wounds you were healed.*
>
> **1 Peter 2:24-25**
> **NASB**

JESUS IS COMING BACK SOON

JOHN 14, REVELATION 22

Even though Jesus went back to heaven to be with God, he promised his friends that he was going to come back for them one day.

Before he left, Jesus told his friends, "In my Father's house are many rooms; and when I leave I am going there to prepare a place for you. So don't worry. After a while, I will come back and take you to be with me in heaven. You can trust God and you can also trust me."

I'm sure Jesus' friends felt really special knowing that one day Jesus would come back and bring them to heaven. But you know what? Jesus' promise is for us too. If you love God and do what he says, Jesus promises to take us to heaven to be with him too.

Just imagine what your room in heaven is going to be like. You can have anything you want in it. Imagine, you

BIBLE ADVENTURE STORIES

can have video games, race cars, stuffed animals, candy, and as much of your favorite food as you want.

Yeah…I know. Since we're not going to have bodies, we probably won't care about that stuff. But, we're still going to feel just as happy as if we were playing a video game marathon, or like if we were munching on our favorite dessert.

Also, imagine being able to see God in heaven. The bible says that in heaven they don't need a sun, because God shines so brightly that he's like the sun shining all day. That's pretty awesome.

The bible also says that in heaven there will never be any crying, sickness or pain…only joy. It's like being at a birthday party that lasts forever.

Now you're probably thinking, "So, when is Jesus coming back?"

Jesus' friends asked him the same thing, too. The truth is we don't know. All that Jesus said was that we need to always be ready, because he can come back at any time.

So, how do you make sure you are ready when Jesus comes? By always loving God and doing everything Jesus taught us to do.

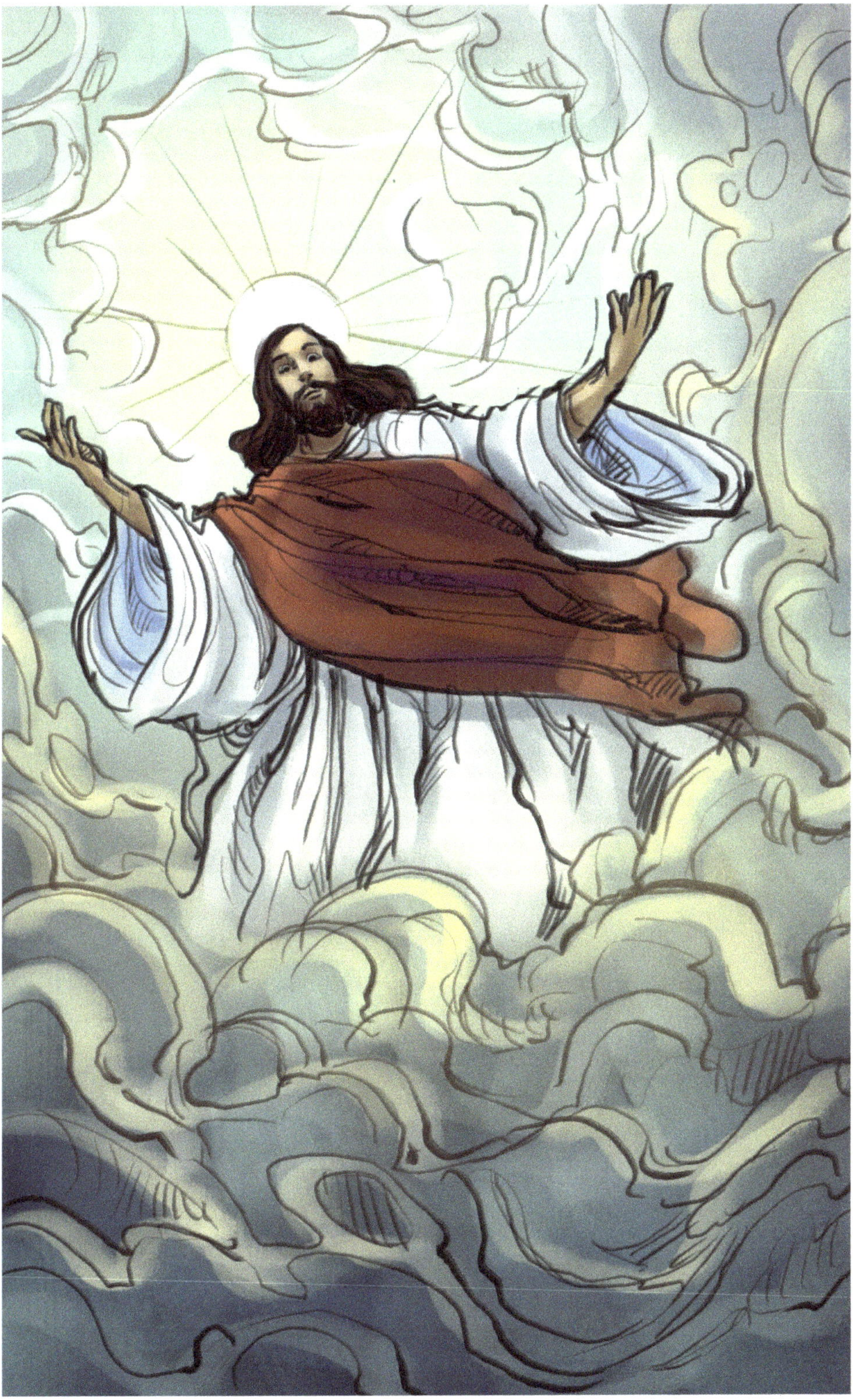

BIBLE ADVENTURE STORIES

And if you do that, Jesus promises that one day, you too, will be with him and God, in heaven, forever.

> *"Behold, I am coming soon! My reward is with me, and I will give to everyone according to what he has done.*
>
> **Revelation 22:12**

COMING SOON...

Bible Adventure Stories Book 2:
25 More Inspiring Stories from the Bible

CPSIA information can be obtained
at www.ICGtesting.com
Printed in the USA
LVHW071508250919
632244LV00029B/543/P